AN EXTRAORDINARY TRUE STORY OF LIBERTY LOST AND LOVE FOUND

By David Gardellin

Bella Vista

Copyright © 2014 by David Gardellin

Background cover photograph was taken in the Dolomite Mountains by Jack Brauer.

See http://www.mountainphotography.com/

1

PROLOGUE

"Before I formed thee in the belly, I knew thee. Before thou camest forth out of the womb, I sanctified thee." Jeremiah 1:5

"My substance was not hid from thee when I was made in secret and curiously wrought in the lowest parts of the earth." Psalms 139:15

Countless priests and ministers feel qualified to describe what happens to us after death. Many years ago, when I was a very young child, I wondered about what lies on the opposite side of the Cartesian scale of life. Is there a conscious 'You' somewhere before you are turned into a physical collection of protoplasmic cells? I dreamt that I was in a place before being born, and God assigned me to choose my parents. Later, he asked if I had found them. I replied that I found the perfect father and mother but they were continents apart and it was inconceivably hopeless they would ever meet. God laughed and said, "Watch".

When the waiter brings the basket of bread and fills the wine glasses and lights the cables, everybody has a story to share. Well, almost everybody. My life has been blessedly uneventful; there's really nothing to tell. But my father's life brings to mind the ancient Chinese curse: "May you live in interesting times."

So when a story is called for, I invariably tell the story of how my father came to America. Many listeners have commented, "That is stranger than fiction. You should write that down." In deference to their entreaty, I am doing just that. Please accept my apology in advance: Having no talent for fiction, I am unable to embellish this story to make it more interesting. I have simply recorded the story of Giuseppe Gardellin as it was told it to me fifty years ago.

File this under The Law of Unintended Consequences:

In 1798, under the threat of a looming war with France, President John Adams signed into law the Alien Enemies and Sedition Acts. This legislation effectively eliminated traditional legal provisions for the issuance of a ***writ of habeas corpus*** and authorized the president to detain, relocate, or deport enemy aliens in time of war. The Franco-American war never materialized but the resulting legislation clung like a barnacle to the ship of state. The threat of a Franco-American war receded and the Enemy Aliens Act faded from the public consciousness but it didn't die; it simply went into a state of suspended animation.

President Franklin Roosevelt reanimated this Frankenstein legislation a century and a half later to justify executive orders 2525, 2526, and 2527. His very elastic interpretation stretched the boundaries of this act to suspend individual rights not just in time of war, but in the circumstance of an *impending* war, incarcerating persons **suspected** of being potentially hostile to the United States a year and a half prior to our entrance into World War II.

The Alien Enemies Act is still in effect today.

This story traces the convoluted path of one man's life, irreversibly altered by entanglement with this obscure 140-year-old piece of legislation. Our story, however, begins earlier even than 1798. Much earlier.

***

In the north of Italy in the Tyrolean Alps, sheep are the visible hands of the celestial clock marking the change of seasons. Every Lenten season, since a time centuries before there was a Lent or an Easter, flocks of sheep and goats make the arduous climb from valley winter pastures to high Alpine meadows, clogging the narrow medieval roads in a cacophony of bleating sheep and barking dogs. Every fall they make the return trip, careening like white water down the narrow ravines.

Otzi strode onto the stage of this celestial choreography, herding sheep on the tides of their annual pilgrimage, until he was brutally murdered one year during the spring migration. His assailants left his body in a narrow ravine high in the Alps. Shortly after this homicide, a snow squall rolled in and gently covered his body in a feathery white shroud.

A thousand years after Otzi's last spring migration, the Egyptians broke ground for the first pyramid.

Two thousand years after Otzi's last spring migration, Moses led the Jews out of captivity.

Three thousand years after Otzi's last spring migration, Jesus celebrated his last Passover with his disciples. Further east, the Chinese set the first brick of their Great Wall in place.

Five thousand years later, in 1991, a couple of hikers discovered his body protruding from a retreating glacier.

The authorities never identified his assailants, but they managed to decipher an extraordinary picture of his life and death. He was part of a complex and specialized society populated by a wide spectrum of artisans and craftsmen. A professional armorer crafted his bow and arrows. Miners, smelters and smiths cooperated to manufacture his copper ice ax. His doctor prescribed the herbs in his medicine bag. He wore insulated clothing, including lederhosen.

And his boots demonstrated astonishingly sophisticated craftsmanship; a composite design of deer skin and bear leather insulated with grass and moss. Four thousand years later, just to the south east in a town called Cittadella was a family that continued the tradition of hand crafting boots.

2

THE SHOE MAKER'S TALE

Cittadella, as the name implies, is a citadel or fortress, perched in the shadows of the Dolomite Mountains in northeastern Italy. Half a kilometer in diameter, it was built in 1220 as a military outpost to protect the city-state of Padua, thirty kilometers to the south.

The walls are 14 to 16 meters tall and are "box masonry": two parallel walls filled with a core of stones and hot slaked lime totaling a thickness of about 2.10 meters. It is surrounded by a moat and accessed by four gates at the cardinal compass points.

The church facing the square in the middle of the town was built at the same time as the walls. The name "Gardellin" is listed in the first volume of the church archives.

Cesare Gardellin was born here July 18, 1882. Giuseppina Bizzotto was born here November 11, 1883. Cesare and Giuseppina were married sometime around 1900.

Cesare Gardellin made sturdy boots for local shepherds, thick leather shoes for farmers, insulated boots with steel hobnails for hikers, and dress shoes for the priest and the banker.

His father, his grandfather, and his great-grandfather made shoes. They made shoes for as long as anyone could remember. According to family legend, the Gardellin family was making shoes centuries before the Roman Empire.

Thursdays were market day. Awnings hung from iron rings set in the castle walls provided shade for the merchant's booths. Every Thursday Cesare hoisted his awning and set up his booth to sell shoes just as generations of Gardellins had done for centuries.

Cesare and Giuseppina's eighth child, their third son, arrived in the usual way on Valentine's Day in 1922. They named him Giuseppe.

From Left to Right: Pia – Guerrino – Ines – Giuseppina (seated) – Pina Nori (on mother's lap) – Irene – Cesare (seated) – Guiseppe (between dad's knees) – Giovanella (in back) – Luciana (in front) – Guglielmo (William). Mariuccia would arrive two years later in September, 1927.

Giuseppe woke up winter mornings with a layer of ice inside the window panes. The boys awoke ahead of the others to load and light the wood stove in the kitchen, and on Sundays the ceramic stove in the parlor as well. Girls were responsible for cooking, cleaning and making sure Papa and the boys had freshly laundered pants and a white shirt ironed and starched every day. The boys also helped in the shoe shop after school.

The dental pattern at the crest of the wall was designed to shield archers while they fired their projectiles. A network of passageways between the inner and outer walls provided archers mobility to quickly relocate along the wall without detection or exposure to enemy fire. By the twentieth century the walls had weakened in places, rendering them unsafe. Climbing on them was strictly forbidden which only enhanced their allure. This enchanted playground was irresistible to Giuseppe and his companions, Bepe Sartori and Feliciano Campus. These self proclaimed "Three Musketeers" routinely flouted the prohibition to climb the parapets in their imaginary battles and adventures.

Giuseppe and sister Pina circa 1929, First Holy Communion, Cittadella, in the Veneto Province of Italy.

The catholic school in Cittadella was the only educational facility in the town so Jewish children attended as well. The requirement for them to take catechism was justified by the rational that it was part of the standard curriculum. However, they were excused from class during their traditional holy days, much to the chagrin of catholic classmates.

The school building included a balcony fitted with a bell that signaled the start of class.

One particularly cold morning the principal pulled the bell rope as usual but the bell was strangely mute. The students continued playing in the school yard. He pulled the rope a little more forcefully. Still silent. The children continued to play. The custodian got a ladder and climbed up to investigate. Someone had apparently turned the bell upside down the previous evening and filled it with water. The bell's tongue was frozen solid. Despite the lack of witnesses or any tangible incriminating evidence, Giuseppe was promptly summoned to the principal's office. His name evidently topped the list of "the usual suspects."

The annual circus visit figured large in Giuseppe's stories of growing up in Cittadella. He was fascinated by exotic animals. One of the circus sharps noticed his fascination with monkeys. The sharp nonchalantly asked if he would like to buy a few. When Giuseppe asked the price, the sharp asked, "How much do you have in your pocket?" By rare coincidence, that was the exact price for a monkey troupe! Giuseppe struck the bargain and proudly marched home with a trio of monkeys tethered on leashes. He set the monkeys in the house and returned to spend the rest of the afternoon at the circus.

Walking home at the end of his enchanted day at the circus, his married sister intercepted him mid route. She advised him it would be extremely prudent for him to go directly to her house for an extended visit without so much as stopping home for a change of clothes. Papa and Mama had arrived home earlier and opened the door to screaming bedlam.

Following a frantic chase, the monkeys were rounded up leaving behind a house littered with shards of china, broken glass and torn curtains. Papa knew exactly what was up and marched the devils back to the circus. Sorry, no refunds.

Another year at the circus, Giuseppe paid hard money for admission to the side-show to marvel at "The Savage Cannibal from Darkest Africa". He was amazed at the sight of such a frightening exotic person. Years later when he traveled abroad and saw a Negro for the first time he realized he had been tricked. The so-called African in the side show was really a white man in burnt cork.

The principle mode of transportation for the Gardellin family was the bicycle. Every summer, Cesare and his family traveled 80 kilometers to the Roman Amphitheater in Verona to see the opera. Father, mother and children old enough to turn the cranks made the pilgrimage by bicycle.

With children setting the pace and panniers filled with lunch and the mandatory bottle of wine, speed was not a particular concern. The trip took the better part of an entire day, the family arriving in time to dine at a restaurant before the overture. After the performance, they rode home through the night, their trip illuminated by the brilliant narrow beam of the carbide lights, arriving home around sunrise the following day.

The Amphitheater in Verona.

As a teenager, Giuseppe explored the surrounding Tyrol by bicycle. Bicycles were incredibly heavy by today's standards and only professional racers had access to bicycles fitted with multiple gears, but a local custom offset the challenge of alpine riding. In those days trucks were not very powerful and relied on very low gearing to make the ascent. This limited their uphill speed to 15 to 20 kilometers per hour.

Truck drivers customarily fastened a short length of knotted rope to the right side of the truck's cargo bed. When a cyclist approached a steep grade, with a few deft peddle strokes he would easily pace alongside a truck gearing down in preparation for the ascent. The cyclist grabbed the rope dangling from the cargo bed and hung on. The truck pulled the cyclist up the grade like the tow rope at a ski resort, the truck plodding slow and steady through a fish ladder of hairpin turns zigzagging through the steep Alpine passes, as the driver adjusted the gearing to the grade. At the summit, even in summer snow lined the sides of the road. The cyclist and the driver could look down at the mountain they had ascended together; green farms dotted with sheep and cows, yellow hay fields and villages like toy-train buildings in the distance.

At the crest, the cyclist uncoupled from the truck and coasted down the other side. At the next climb, the cyclist would latch onto the truck again and so on. At mid-day the driver stopped at a café or restaurant. The cyclist was obligated by custom to reciprocate the favor and treat the driver to lunch and conversation in exchange for the tow. Giuseppe traveled extensively by bicycle and occasionally by train. He traversed the world by steamship. He wouldn't drive an automobile until he was well into his forties, and then only under duress.

3

TYROLEAN POLITICS

In 218 BC, Hannibal marched his war elephants over the Alps en route to Rome. Hannibal was a brilliant strategist. He slaughtered Roman soldiers by the tens of thousands. But the Roman Dictator Fabius Maximus thwarted his grand design to capture Rome. Fabius Maximus' agnomen was *"Cunctator"* which means "the delayer." Initially a pejorative, until Romans saw that they were winning the war at less cost in lives and money. Then the title morphed into a badge of honor.

The poor man's answer to the Blitzkrieg, Fabian strategy is classic Tyrolean thinking; avoid direct confrontation and employ guerilla tactics to bleed your nemesis to death through a protracted war of attrition. If history is any indication, George Washington and Ho Chi Min were well read concerning Fabius Maximus.

In 1162 AD, Barbarossa and his 100,000 German soldiers poured over the Alps and captured the Lombard region. So he thought. The supposed capture was plagued by an unrelenting series of revolts and skirmishes. Barbarossa returned and recaptured the region again. But an unending series of revolts eventually bled his resources dry. Returning home, he decided that it would be far easier to unite Germany instead.

In 1494 AD, the Medici's, led by Pope Leo X, subdued the Florentine Republic. Within a few decades the last Medici was dead and Florence flourished.

In the late 1920s, Germanic barbarians and Roman centurions were resurrected as Nazis and Fascists, with the communists struggling for a foothold as well. On Sundays the family listened to the radio in the parlor. Sometimes they listened to stations from Rome; often they listened to stations from Innsbruck; less than half as far as Rome the station came in much clearer. News about the Nazis, Fascists and communists dominated the air waves in the 1920s and 1930s.

Giuseppe frequently heard Hitler and Mussolini delivering speeches on the radio. One year his scout troop won a contest. The prize was a train trip to Germany to attend a rally to hear Hitler deliver a speech in person. Giuseppe and his companions were excited to make the trip but were more interested in ogling German 'Fraulines' than listening to German politicians. Years later Giuseppe would talk about the Nazi rally, the spectacular parades, the goose stepping devotees and torchlight processions. Giuseppe warned that a sea of waving flags and cheering crowds is inevitably the harbinger of an impending load of horseshit.

In the Tyrolean mindset, La famiglia è il prima; the family is first. Naturally you are a citizen of a town. You might be, by way of example, from Cittadella. At a larger level of magnification, you are from the Veneto region. Finally, at the maximum level of magnification, you are a Tyrolean. That's as far as it goes. The concept of "Italy" is an abstraction, like saying you are a part of the Milky Way. Intellectually you grasp the concept but it has no tangible application in your daily life.

Cesare and Giuseppina didn't speak "Italian." They spoke "Tyrolean" a dialect that, like the local cuisine, is a hash of Italian and German. In Cittadella, Cesare's workday frequently ended at the local cafe for pinochle, grappa (a type of brandy indigenous to the region), gossip and friendly banter. If someone wandered into the café speaking Italian, the café fell silent. The strangers were obviously either tax collectors or secret police.

With Italy caught between the jaws of the Fascists on one side and the Communists on the other, Cesare and his fellow tradesmen viewed both extremes with disdain and trepidation. Giuseppe once related a joke popular in the Tyrol at the time; the punch line portrayed Mussolini as a mound of rabbit shit. Jokes of this sort were shared only among trusted friends; the Fascists had ears everywhere.

Giuseppe explained Fascist-Nazi politics: Fascists don't outlaw collective bargaining. They pass "legislation to prevent service disruptions." Union agitators are assassinated but the trains run on time.

Fascists don't confiscate guns; they pass "public safety legislation". A private citizen technically can have title to a firearm, but has to store it at the local police station and sign out for it whenever he is inclined to embark on a day of duck hunting.

When Cesare's first daughter was born, he purchased a walnut tree from a local farmer. As each girl married, he contracted a local cabinet maker to transform the wood into a bed for her trousseau.

The cheese on the dinner table in the Gardellin household came from a local dairy farm. Sausage came from the butcher shop down the street. Wine came from vineyards no further than Alto Adage. Beer was brewed by a brewery in town. Clothes were made by the local tailor and seamstress.

By the 1930s, the economics of mass production sounded the death knell for cottage craftsmen. A bed was no longer made from a tree the slumberer had climbed in her youth. Bespoke shoes fell out of fashion; shoes were mass produced in an anonymous factory hundreds of kilometers away.

After more generations than anyone could count, Cesare had the unenviable task of informing his sons that the business was finished. The end of the craft tradition and the economic malaise of the Great Depression left the Gardellin sons with few options.

Giuseppe's oldest brother Guglielmo immigrated to Argentina to work for Cesare's brother who had an established business there. Following a falling out with his uncle, Guglielmo ended up working at the Fiat factory in Buenos Aires.

Giuseppe's other brother, Guerrino, joined the priesthood. Shortly after his ordination, Guerrino became a missionary to the Indians who live high in the Peruvian mountains.

He toiled for five decades in the thin, cold air in one of the poorest places on Earth. In one of his letters to Giuseppe he writes that on a typical Sunday the collection basket averages about $20 in today's currency. He is extraordinarily happy. A decade after beginning his mission, he wrote home boasting that he now had a motor vehicle for making his parish rounds. The letter included a photograph of him sitting proudly on a rusty motorcycle.

Guglielmo and Guerrino weren't the only ones to immigrate from Cittadella to the New World in search of a livelihood. Their sister Giovanella's best friend married a man named 'Scringi.' The girls had a tearful farewell when Mr and Mrs Scringi immigrated to America where he had arranged to work in the coal mines near Hazleton, PA.

As 1937 wound down, newspaper headlines were trumpeting Italian victories in the war in Ethiopia and Italy's withdrawal from the League of Nations. In Cittadella the year closed quietly. In the Church on the central square, the Nativity scene appeared in the nave to the left of the sacristy, just as it did every year. The three wise men appeared in the Nativity scene weeks later on the Feast of the Epiphany on January 6th. In the Tyrol, exchanging gifts coincides with the day the Magi presented gifts to Jesus, so the Epiphany more closely resembles American Christmas with decorations and the traditional family dinner.

The Gardellin family celebrated the Epiphany that year at Giuseppe's sister Ines's house, one block from their house through the south gate of the castle. Ines's husband Ettorre was enjoying a rare visit with his family. Ettorre was in his mid-thirties; he was the purser on the Luxury Liner *Conte Biancamano* of the Italian Lines. (Later renamed 'Lloyd Sabaudo,' and still later resuming the original 'Italian Lines' name).

Ines and Ettorre's house was filled with food, presents, parents, brothers, sisters, cousins and friends crowded around the dining room table and the ceramic stove in the parlor. Fifteen year old Giuseppe listened spellbound as Ettorre, seated at the head of the table, regaled his guests with stories about his adventures in China, India and America. He gossiped about the foibles and follies of the super rich and the celebrity passengers on the ship. Exotic oriental souvenirs lined the shelves of the kitchen dresser behind him.

Ettorre asked Giuseppe what he had been doing since he finished school.

Giuseppe responded, "I help father in the shop. And I have a job."

Ettorre asked, "What kind of job?"

"At the hospital."

"What are you doing in the hospital?"

"I'm an orderly. Making beds, serving meals, mopping floors, sweeping."

"Do you like it?"

"It's depressing. You're around sick people all day. Or people who are dying. I don't know how the nurses do it year after year. And it pays a few lire a week, peanuts."

"If you're going to make beds and serve meals, why don't you come to work on the ship? You'd be doing the same thing, but you'd be serving happy people who just party all day. You'd make more money. You'd have no living expenses; the shipping company provides accommodations and food. And I'm talking great food like you've never tasted in your life."

Giuseppe's mother, who had been having an animated conversation with Ines, halted her conversation in mid sentence and shot Ettorre an angry glance. He pretended not to notice.

Giuseppe asked, "Do you think I really could?"

Ettorre answered, "Sure. It would be the education of a life time. If you're serious, ask your father."

Later that night Giuseppe's parents had a hushed conversation in their darkened bedroom. At one point Cesare said to his wife, "Why not? What's the boy going to do here? There's no future in the shoe shop. There are no jobs here. Better he should be far away and safe in the middle of the ocean than have Mussolini draft him for his next African adventure. Besides, Ettorre will keep an eye on him."

Brother-in-law pulled a few strings and Giuseppe landed a job that promised travel, adventure and, if not riches, at least a steady paycheck. So it was that on a blustery, rainy day in February 1938, Cesare, Ettorre and Giuseppe rode in a hired car 30 kilometers to the train station in Padua. Standing stoically on the train platform, Cesare didn't smile or cry; he stood very upright and formal as Ettorre and Giuseppe climbed the steps into the train carriage and he forced a smile as he waved to Giuseppe through the rain streaked window. The train lurched forward and began picking up speed, huffing clouds of white smoke. He stood watching the train fade into the distance until the sound of the bell died away and nothing remained but a smoke plume like a black smudge on the horizon. A week before his sixteenth birthday, Giuseppe became a steward on the Italian Liner *Conte Biancamano*.

4

THE SAILOR'S TALE

The culture on Italian luxury liners was a mix of navy discipline and Italian hospitality. Crew members arrived for inspection at the start of each shift on-time, shoes spit-shined, white shirt pressed and starched, creases in pants, and white gloves spotless. The Italian Lines provided passengers from the highest echelon of society a travel experience congruent with the gentile sophistication they took for granted in their mansions and country estates.

Giuseppe's initial shipboard duties were a mix of bell hop, room service and busboy, ferrying luggage, making beds and waiting tables.

One afternoon, as the Conte Biancamano steamed towards the equator, brilliant afternoon sunlight gleaming off the white superstructure made the ship look incongruously like a snow capped mountain floating through a sweltering tropical ocean. Just off the deck next to the swimming pool, the head steward was listening stoically to one of the waiters taking a break from serving drinks pool side. The waiter was in a foul mood, "Every afternoon the women from first class descend with their children and turn the place into a hen house, and every one of them is the Queen of the Swamp. I have more prima donnas than La Scalla. All afternoon it's 'get me a drink. Bring me a fresh towel. Bring me something to eat.' They

First Class Lounge on the Conte Biancamano

complain the service isn't fast enough. They complain about everything. The way they tip makes Scrooge look like a spendthrift."

The head steward thought for a moment, and then replied, "Maybe we could have some fun with this. We could perform a kind of scientific experiment."

"What did you have in mind?"

"Where's that new kid? The one from the Veneto region?"

"Ettore's brother-in-law?"

"Yes, him. Why don't we 'promote' him to pool side for an afternoon?"

"You're going to throw the cricket into that jar of scorpions? That's heartless. He's barely sixteen."

"Let's see what happens."

The following afternoon, numerous crew members found some pretext to be on the deck overlooking the pool. They peered over the railing and saw Giuseppe serving drinks, bringing towels...and calmly ordering the passengers about. They watched in amusement as Giuseppe approached a red haired woman in a bathing suit lounging with a book in a deck chair next to the pool.

"Signora, you must move."

"I beg your pardon, young man?"

"You've been in the sun for hours. We are just a few degrees from the equator. This isn't like the sun on Brighton Beach or Atlantic City. At this latitude you'll have second degree burns before you realize it. Look at your arms and shoulders already. You should move into the shade now. Why don't you join the three ladies at that table over there in the shade? They love to play bridge; you'll make a foursome."

She gently closed her book, got up from the lounge chair and disappeared into a bouquet of umbrellas as quietly as a leopard vanishing into the jungle canopy.

As he walked past the pool with a tray of drinks a pair of teenage girls swam across the pool and began splashing him with water. He admonished them with mock seriousness, "Look at what you've done! Now my shirt is wrinkled, what a mess! I'm going to report you!" The girls laughed at him. One of them replied, "I know how to iron. Where's your cabin? I'll come down later and starch it for you."

After serving drinks to a 40-something woman sitting off to one side of the pool deck, she discretely folded a bill in half and slid it into his breast pock, patting it several times.

After watching this spectacle at the pool side, his fellow crewmen nicknamed him "Il Gallo" (The Rooster). When one of the crewmen asked Ettorre about his brother-in-law he replied, "He's used to women. He has seven sisters that all dote on him."

The Head Steward's noticed that Giuseppe consistently garnered generous tips from well-to-do matrons. He made a calculated decision to have him fitted with first class dining livery including jacket with tails.

As a first class waiter, Giuseppe's training included a mind-numbing array of minutiae related to table setting, seating arrangements, the sequence of courses and beverages, the arrangement of eating utensils, china, cutlery, crystal, and obscure specialized dishes and utensils that ordinary mortals see on rare occasions. This training imbued him with a lifelong ability to mesh seamlessly with people from every station in life and an uncanny ability to quickly discern class from wealth.

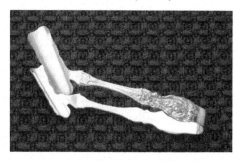

Correctly identify this utensil and you might quality to wait table in first class dining. The answer is on the next page.

In addition to details of protocol, stewards were expected to converse with guests in their own language. Giuseppe quickly learned conversational Spanish, French, German, and English in addition to Italian. Giuseppe's natural linguistic ability lent itself to some interesting situations. The Captain had a particular fondness for one of the Spanish passengers with whom he was having an affair. They were conversing intimately while Giuseppe was in the room when it suddenly occurred to the Captain that Giuseppe might be fluent in Spanish. When he inquired if this was in fact the case, Giuseppe adroitly replied, "I understand it very well but don't speak a word of it," a response that instantly elevated him in the Captain's graces and resulted in a notable increase in his next paycheck.

Giuseppe traveled to seaports throughout Europe, North and South America, and Asia.

In Shanghai, Giuseppe and his uncle hired a rickshaw for the afternoon to see the sights. After several hours of touring, eating and drinking, the rickshaw came to an abrupt halt in a particularly seedy part of town. At this point the driver informed his passengers of a sudden and substantial price increase in the fare back to the ship. Giuseppe immediately contested the point, his voice rising in pitch and volume, resonating off the closely packed buildings until his brother-in-law drew his attention to the crowd of sinister looking men that had quietly gravitated around the rickshaw. He suggested that a dignified concession would be a more prudent response to their situation.

The utensil shown on the previous page is an asparagus tongs. In case you were wondering.

Giuseppe observed firsthand the workings of British colonialism in India. A pair of English policemen was walking along the sidewalk when a native walking the opposite direction refused to yield to them. Without hesitating they took out their nightsticks and beat him unconscious. This was not uncommon in India at that time. But despite the beatings, Indian boys continued taunting the British police daily. The British police could beat Indians until their arms fell off but in the end there would be plenty of Indians standing. The ultimate conclusion of this contest was only a matter of time and both the British and the Indians understood this. Giuseppe's confidence in the ultimate triumph of India's desire for independence was reinforced when he met Mahatma Gandhi as a passenger on his ship.

5

STORM CLOUDS ON THE HORIZON

During the summer of 1939 the *Conte Biancamano* was on a routine trip to Valparaiso, Chile. The white behemoth slid gracefully through the locks in the Panama Canal. Some of the passengers stood at the railing with cameras taking pictures of the locks and winches that lifted and nudged the vessel gently up and over the isthmus.

As the ship cleared the last lock at the west end of the labyrinth one of the canal engineers watched the white vessel glide past. He could hear the orchestra playing the latest jazz tunes as the ship glided serenely into the Pacific Ocean towards the horizon. The music slowly died away and nothing could be seen but the black smoke plume from the funnels.

As night fell and the *Conte Biancamano* steamed South towards Valparaiso, passengers in the lounge listened anxiously to news on the short wave radio. Storm clouds were gathering over Europe. Hitler and Stalin signed a non-aggression pact, effectively codifying the vivisection of Europe.

At the same time, a different kind of storm was brewing. That night on the bridge the navigator made it a point to record the barometer reading every hour, neatly plotting the readings. The barometer was taking a nose dive. Just before midnight, he knocked on the Captain's cabin door and showed him the graph. The Captain ordered a few degrees change in course and jotted down instructions for the crew before he went back to sleep.

By the time the day crew reported for breakfast the next morning new orders from the Captain had already been posted. That morning the swimming pool was drained and covered. Deck chairs and tables were brought in and stowed. During routine room service, crew members were instructed to check that all the porthole windows were closed and locked securely. Crewmen with big wrenches retightened the bolts on the cargo hatch covers.

By late afternoon, intervals of bright sunshine alternated with rain squalls, large drops of rain splattering against the windows. By nightfall, the rain had intensified and the wind had increased to a steady wail and the ship began rocking more than Giuseppe was used to. The next day the typhoon was at full force with rain pelting the ship and the wind swelling to an unrelenting shriek with waves crashing over the bow. The dining rooms were virtually deserted, only the most hardy and seasoned travelers seated for meals. Most of the passengers retreated to their staterooms, ordering meals from room service which consisted almost universally of hot tea and dry toast. It was all Giuseppe and his fellow stewards could manage without scalding themselves; climbing the stairwell with a try laden with the hot teapot and plates of food into a long windowless hallway that suddenly lurched upwards so that it was like hiking up a steep hill and then, as the ship crested the wave, the floor under his feet would tip forward with a sickening lunge and he had to hold the tray with one hand and grab the railing with the other to keep from sliding forward. In the ballroom, the cable that anchored the grand piano to the iron ring in the floor snapped from the jarring. The piano began a slow shimmy that grew into a larger undulation, sliding back and forth the length of the ballroom until it crashed into one of the tables and one of the legs snapped off. The music program was cancelled for the evening.

At midmorning of the third day the Chief Engineer arrived on the bridge and told the Captain that he'd better come down and take a look below decks. The Captain and Chief Engineer left the bridge and disappeared down into the stairwell, descending the spiral to the lowest deck and working their way forward into the bow. They stopped at one point in the dark cramped space and the Chief Engineer took his flashlight and pointed it towards the inside of the hull.

"There." said the Chief Engineer, "It's those four plates there. You can see the water leaking through the seam every time the ship dives into a wave. It looks like that entire row of rivets has stretched. One millimeter. Maybe two. It started this morning as a trickle."

"How fast is it leaking?"

"I'd estimate twenty liters a minute right now. The pumps can handle it at the moment but it's increasing steadily. At this rate it'll be over 50 by midnight. If a few more rivets start to quit, it could get ugly."

"Ok, have somebody check it every hour and give me a report. The barometer is starting to pick back up a little so this storm should ease off by late tomorrow."

The typhoon began tapering off by noon the following day, and the Conte Biancamano made it to Valparaiso without further incident. But several of the riveted plates comprising the hull suffered severe damage. The Captain wasn't taking any chances, ordering the ship into dry dock for repairs. By the time repairs were complete and the tug boats gently nudged her into position at dockside, she was weeks behind schedule. By sunrise hundreds of passengers were already cued in line in a late winter drizzle waiting to board. When the gang plank was lowered, they quickly surged forward to escape the cold wind sweeping down the wharf. The stevedores worked double-time loading coal, food, and baggage.

Giuseppe darted back and forth, steering carts filled with luggage and guiding passengers to their state rooms. He accompanied a very distinguished woman with grey hair and English clothes to her first class cabin. The luggage cart was loaded with a steamer trunk and half dozen suitcases, topped with a small cage housing a yellow finch. The bird flitted fitfully side to side on his perch. Giuseppe could barely see over the baggage to steer the cart. After unloading the luggage in her cabin, he astutely noted she was a generous tipper.

By mid-afternoon, the gangplank had been hauled up. The tug boats put their shoulders to the hull and turned the white liner towards the open sea. As soon as the tugs swung free, the Captain swung the handles on the telegraph, clanging, calling for full steam.

Giuseppe had just ensconced the last passenger into his stateroom. The head steward spotted him in the hallway. "Beppe! Beppe! The ice sculptor needs ice to carve the center piece for tonight's dinner. Run down to the freezer. Start with a couple of blocks and see how much he needs." Giuseppe scurried to the freezer. He unhooked a pair of tongs hanging inside the door. He caught one of the translucent blocks firmly in the iron pincers, yanked it from its place and turned back towards the dining room. He could feel the deck throbbing under his feet as the engines wound up to full speed. He swayed to keep his footing as he balanced the ice with the ship rolling and pitching. After numerous trips with the ice, Giuseppe had a short respite and dinner break before waiting tables and delivering meals for room service. When Giuseppe's shift was over he collapsed into his bunk and fell into a deep sleep.

As night fell and the *Conte Biancamano* steamed north on her voyage to Genoa, passengers in the lounge listened anxiously to even more alarming news on the short wave radio. Hitler had unleashed the blitzkrieg on Poland. On September 3, 1939, while the liner *Il Conte Biancamano* was in transit in the Panama Canal at Cristobal, Great Britain and France declared war on Germany. The US Navy and Coast Guard bared any further movement of German or Italian ships in US ports. All ships flying Axis colors in territorial waters were seized. The crews were detained under house arrest by the "U.S. Neutrality Patrol" the name of which certainly constitutes a textbook example of Orwellian government-speak.

Surely this was a temporary glitch. Things would be sorted out quickly. The Wehrmacht would stream roll over the Polish Army. In a few days, a couple weeks at most, it would be a fait accompli. England would issue a statement of condemnation and then back down. America would issue another declaration of neutrality. Everything would be back to normal. They would resume their journey home to Genoa. Days stretched into weeks. Weeks stretched into months. With each passing day, small knots of passengers disembarked to fend for themselves in Panama.

The passengers gone, there were no beds to make in the empty staterooms. The dining rooms fell silent. There were no meals to serve, no ice sculptures to carve. There were no drinks to serve on the sun deck. Empty chairs surrounded the glistening swimming pool. The ballroom was silent except for the hum of a vacuum cleaner. There were no dancers for the orchestra to entertain. There were no customers in the barber shop. The movie theater was dark and silent.

For the eighteen months there was little to do beyond rudimentary maintenance. Days were taken up reading the newspaper and listening to the radio.

On February 14, 1940, Giuseppe celebrated his 17th birthday under house arrest on the Conte Biancamano.

On February 14, 1941, Giuseppe celebrated his 18th birthday under house arrest on the Conte Biancamano.

On March 3, 1941, nine months before Pearl Harbor and a US declaration of war, the US Navy and Coast Guard moved against Italian ships. In all, 28 Italian ships were confiscated by the Coast Guard, accusing the crews of sabotage and arresting them. There were 483 Italian crewmen taken into custody. They were soon joined by a group of German seamen, including the *Columbus* crew, and the Italian Pavilion employees from the 1939 New York World's Fair were added to the mix. In all, nearly 1,700 Axis noncombatants faced an uncertain future in a country not yet at war. In 1941, with America not yet at war, no one in the Navy, Coast Guard or the State Department knew the precise legal status of the crew or what should be done with them

In December, 1941 the *Conte Biancamano* was converted to a troop ship and commissioned in the United States Navy as the USS Hermitage.

The Alien and Sedition Acts have bedeviled American politics and jurisprudence since being signed into law in 1798. When the Navy arrested the crew, they were initially incarcerated at Fort Leavenworth Federal Penitentiary in Kansas. However, prison officials soon raised questions about the legality of incarcerating people who hadn't been charged with any crime. The military dodged thorny constitutional questions by simply transferring detainees to the custody of Immigration and Naturalization Service. They washed their hands of the whole affair.

Ultimately, the Immigration and Naturalization Service had to deal with 16,845 Japanese, 10,905 Germans, and 3,278 Italians, all labeled "dangerous aliens." This was an influx of prisoners they hadn't anticipated and with whom they were ill prepared to cope.

The crew from the Conte Biancamano was transferred to Ellis Island, which had been converted from an immigration station into a prison facility. They were incarcerated there for approximately two months.

With terribly crowded conditions they were jailed with virtually no amenities and stripped of any rights. These episodes preceded U.S. entry into World War II by more than two years and marked the beginning of the detention and internment of noncombatants in the global conflict. They also initiated an elaborate program of censoring the personal and business mail of detainees and internees of war.

6

CHE BELLA VISTA

In 1941, the INS acquired two military installations from the War Department: Fort Missoula, four miles southeast of Missoula, Montana and Fort Lincoln, near Bismarck, North Dakota. It expanded them into detention stations that, with double bunking, could each hold more than two thousand prisoners.

Fort Missoula started life in June of 1877 as an outpost for cavalry troops sent to defend homesteaders against Indian attack. In World War I it served as a training camp for mechanics under the direction of the military and Montana State University at Missoula. In the 1930's the government used it for a district office for the Civilian Conservation Corporation.

Fort Missoula was nestled in a scenic, lush valley. One detainee described the setting: "To the southwest was a mountain range. To the east were battlefields where, it is said, the Bitterroot River ran red with blood during the Indian wars. Now there were fish in the clear cold water which flowed from the mountains which were still covered with snow. Wild flowers carpeted the fields and there were even some purple iris bordering the barracks planted by someone who had lived there earlier. It was a quiet, beautiful place."

That quiet, beautiful place came alive with the sounds of activity beginning in mid-April 1941 as the Immigration Service worked feverishly to prepare the camp for the arrival of a thousand seamen. It was a huge task that fell to Nick Collaer, an Immigration Service officer from Texas who was named supervisor of alien detentions at Missoula. There were several existing buildings on the grounds, but many had to be adapted for the special needs of the detainees. The Immigration Service required headquarters, offices, barracks, warehouses, dining halls, hospital, dental clinic, garages, maintenance shops, firehouse, fence and guard towers.

When the Italian detainees arrived for the first time, they called the place "Che Bella Vista," and the name stuck throughout its tenure as a concentration camp.

After enduring the harsh conditions at Ellis Island, on May 9, 1941, the Italian detainees were loaded onto trains with small barred windows. After three days in the cramped dark train cars, the Italian detainees arrived at Fort Missoula, Montana. Although not charged with any crime they were detained indefinitely without writ of habeas corpus

Six months later, on December 7, 1941 the Japanese attacked Pearl Harbor. Within hours the United States declared war on Japan and Germany, and Franklin Roosevelt signed executive orders 2525, 2526 and 2527, authorizing the permanent detention of foreign citizens under the aegis of the Enemy Aliens Act of 1798.

Now it was official.

Giuseppe and the other Italian crewmen from the Comte Biancamano would soon have company. Thousands of Japanese "dangerous aliens" living in California, many with sons serving in the US Military, were summarily rounded up, stripped of businesses and homes, and shipped to Fort Missoula.

On 14-February-1942, Giuseppe celebrated his nineteenth birthday at the Fort Missoula concentration camp. During two and a half years of interment, Giuseppe gleaned newspapers and magazines for a picture of what life was like for American teenagers. Seemingly, the teens' primary concern was whether their parents would let them use the family car on prom night. He, on the other hand, was not able to call a girl on the phone.

Giuseppe watching a soccer game at Fort Missoula.

Then Jim Menager became entangled with the Fort Missoula concentration camp and its inmates. Jim Menager was one of those people imbued with that nebulous quality called "charm;" one of those extraordinary individuals that everyone from every station in life likes instinctively. He had an imbued habit of listening to people. He accomplished extraordinary things by making other people think it was their idea. Had he pursued a carrier in sales, he no doubt would have owned a car dealership or a major department store by this point in his career. But what Jim Menager chose to promote was not cars or appliances, but God. With his intellectual gifts, he naturally gravitated to the Jesuit order. The Fort Missoula Concentration Camp had a chapel and the detainees attended mass every Sunday. Each Sunday Father Jim Menager drove forty miles from St Ignatius to Fort Missoula to say mass, which is how he met Giuseppe, Ettorre, and numerous other Italian detainees.

After mass, Jim Menager would have breakfast with the detainees. He asked one of the detainees about life at Fort Missoula. The internee responded: "Si mangia, si veve e si dorme – e questro e la vita a Bella Vista." (We eat, we drink, and we sleep; this is life at Bella Vista.) Jim quickly recognized the danger of enforced idleness. He approached Nick Collaer to voice his concerns; Collaer had similar reservations. Collaer was intelligent enough to recognize the emotional toll that interminable boredom was taking on the prisoners in his charge and the threat that idleness posed to the security of his detention camp. At the same time he was pragmatic enough to recognize the devastating effect the draft was having on farmers and lumber companies unable to harvest crops and trees for the want of workers. Typical was the situation in Phillips County, Montana. By early March 1942 nearly a thousand men had been inducted into the armed forces and another thousand had left to work in war materials industries on the west coast. At the same time, beet producers had contracted to seed a crop 25% larger than the 1941 harvest. Although it literally took an act of congress, with cooperation from Montana's governor and representatives in Washington D.C., Jim Menager and Nick Collaer were able to initiate a work parole program for the internees at Fort Missoula. Jim Menager was the initial Parole Officer for this program. Giuseppe volunteered to work at the Kaniksu Forest lumber camp in the Idaho Panhandle. No one was forced to work.

On the appointed day, Giuseppe and the rest of the lumber crew assembled after breakfast in front of the dining hall. Two trucks fitted with makeshift benches rolled up in front of the hall. As a list of names was called out each man climbed the tail gate into the cargo bed. It was early enough in the day that the grass was still wet as a guard swung open the gate and the trucks rolled towards the main road. With nothing but a sea of grass surrounding the camp, the mountains on the horizon looked close enough to reach with a short walk, but the trucks drove across the high plateau for over an hour before the road started to climb. The trucks lurched each time the driver shifted into a lower gear and gunned the engine for the next ascent. It was a bright sunny day with a clear blue sky and a line of clouds like a line of white elephants on the western horizon. By eleven o'clock the day began to feel hot and dust from the road settled on the passengers in the open cargo beds.

The road snaked through the mountains along a twisting corridor of pine trees. By late afternoon the shadows of the trees shaded the passengers in the trucks. At one point they drove along a river and the men could look over the guard trail and see the river below and they could hear the water rushing over the rocks.

The trucks turned off the highway onto a narrow gravel road. Shafts of sunlight angled through the trees illuminating a thick carpet of pine needles on the forest floor.

The tucks rolled down a gulley and across a wooden bridge. The boards rumbled like distant thunder on a summer afternoon. Below the bridge a galaxy of yellow pollen slowly revolved on the still black water. The air was heavy with the smell of pine sap. By early evening the trucks arrived at the lumber camp, a small cluster of white washed buildings, Spartan, but neat and clean. There was no fence.

The next morning the detainees were paired with veteran loggers. Giuseppe learned the subtle arts of de-branching, sawing, and learning how to fell a tree in the right direction, how to work the two-man saw so the weight of the tree didn't bind it up, and how to hone the edges of a double bladed ax. After two years of enforced idleness, Giuseppe had something to do. Something productive.

Giuseppe was quickly absorbed into an exotic tribe unlike any that he had ever met in his prior travels. Lumberjacks and cattle ranchers worked at dangerous jobs with aplomb whether it was minus 40 or plus 90 degrees. They were irreverent men who suffered fools poorly and whose daily conversation was peppered with such colorful profanity that even the sailors were favorably impressed. One day at dinner, one of the lumberjacks asked Giuseppe why his fellow crewmen from the Conte Biancamano called him "Il Gallo". Giuseppe tried to explain that it was a nickname but, not knowing the English word for 'rooster' he translated it as 'the bull of the chicken' inspiring much laughter and amusement from his new American friends.

Aside from the lack of a girlfriend, no small setback, he thought his circumstances much improved.

Nick Collaer believed in transparent relations with the neighboring community. He took the initiative to address town councils and newspapers in the surrounding communities, explaining that the internees in his custody were neither criminals nor enemy combatants. The internees didn't wear prison garb. Giuseppe was surprised at the difference between his treatment at the hands of the American Government and the way American citizens treated him. The men in the logging crew treated him like a friend. When he went to Bonners Ferry to pick up supplies and cash his check (accompanied by the ever present guard) townspeople treated him kindly with no sign of resentment or hostility.

All of Giuseppe's assumptions about his host country were being rudely turned inside-out; he found himself in the uncomfortable position of having to reexamine everything that he thought he knew about America. This is Giuseppe's genius. Despite a visceral disdain for the American Government, which continued pretty much unabated throughout his life, he saw the remarkable qualities of American people. He genuinely admired the independent spirit of the American rancher and lumberjack. Despite seeing America from no other vantage point than as a prisoner, he was able to perceive and appreciate the remarkable freedoms that Americans enjoy.

He was beginning to master the choreography of the two-man saw and the double-bladed ax with grace and speed.

Then, in July 1943 Giuseppe had unexpected visitors. A pair of somber faced men in grey suits showed up at the lumber camp accompanied by guards from Fort Missoula. They were from the Office of Strategic Services (OSS), forerunner to the CIA. The men had little trouble securing a private room for a discussion with Giuseppe.

They asked a lot of questions. Where did he grow up? How many languages could he speak? Which cities in Europe and Asia was he familiar with? Did he still have contacts in these cities? How did he feel about Mussolini? How were they treating him at the concentration camp? What did he think about America?

After a long interview, he was directed to wait outside. Several minutes later he was called back. Would he like to go to school? This was a special school, near Washington DC. He would be an American secret agent. He would make a great contribution to the American war effort. Giuseppe enthusiastically agreed. At the conclusion of the meeting they shook hands.

When Giuseppe caught up with Ettorre, he enthusiastically told him about his new-found vocation in the spy business. Ettorre listened silently, his face darkening like an eclipse. After a moment of silence, he reached out and with his palm he gave Giuseppe a knock on the side of his head and simply said, "Stupido!"

"How many times have I told you? Never volunteer for shit! Fascisti, Communista, Nazis, Republicans, Democrats. They're all horse's asses and whores looking out for themselves. How am I supposed to explain this to your sister? What do I tell your mother and father? If I write to them saying where you went, the censors will cut it out. They won't allow you to communicate with anybody, not even your parents. What are Cesare and Josephina going to think when they don't hear from you? And when they write and ask me what's happening, they get a letter back that looks like Swiss cheese?"

A few days later Ettorre and Father Jim Menager rode silently with Giuseppe in the back of the truck to the Fort Missoula train station. They stood wordlessly on the platform in the morning light, the scent of pine trees in the air. When the locomotive lumbered up next to the platform hissing steam and bell clanging, Ettorre and Giuseppe hugged and kissed each other on the check. The INS men put handcuffs on Giuseppe along with eight other detainees form Fort Missoula and herded them up the steps into the passenger car. Ettorre watched silently as the car doors slammed shut. The train slid away from the platform and gradually shrank to a dot on the horizon. The smoke from the locomotive quickly vanished in the summer breeze.

Giuseppe had ample time as he rode east towards Washington to muse on his new carrier path. Marvel Comic pictures of life as a secret agent played out on the movie screen of his imagination, images of traveling with a miniature camera or a secret shortwave radio hidden in a shaving kit.

The OSS file for Giuseppe Gardellin includes a time-stamped receipt for "delivery of one enemy alien," showing that

Giuseppe arrived at his new campus at 9:50 AM, Monday 19-July-1943, at the Office of Strategic Services, Building – Q, Washington DC. Nine internees from the Fort Missoula Concentration Camp were assigned the code name "Bison Group."

It was short, intense curriculum, matriculation to graduation spanning all of three weeks. It doesn't take long to transform someone with a modicum of mechanical aptitude into a reasonably proficient bomb maker. Subject matter included the art of connecting plastic explosives and blasting caps, concealing plastic explosives inside ordinary objects like a guitar or wrapping them in butcher paper and mixing them in with a basket of groceries. In his lab sessions he learned to make a detonation timer from a pocket watch, how to place shrapnel around the explosive for maximum casualties and how to sequence multiple timed explosions to create an avalanche of panic. His curriculum was a cram-course in mental flexibility. Between bomb making lectures, his instructors presented ingenious weapons created by prison inmates: sundry objects like a toothbrush or eyeglass frames refashioned into lethal weapons. Giuseppe was a quick study and graduated with stellar marks.

Then, in one critical moment, the weed seed of a small misunderstanding began to germinate.

Friday morning August 6, 1943, dawned hot and grew steadily more oppressive. By mid afternoon, heat waves rose from the city streets like a chimera. The flags outside the office buildings hung limp in the still air. The granite faced buildings lining the street became a desert canyon in the afternoon glare.

Inside Building-Q the harsh sunlight poured in the open windows and glared off the polished terrazzo corridors floors. The drone of hundreds of desk fans permeated the air, accompanied by the clacking of typewriters periodically punctuated by the chime of tiny bells marking the end of each line of text. In the hallway outside the conference room assigned to the Bison Group, the murmuring of voices emanated through the open transom.

It was time to launch the operation, and Lieutenant William Downey was explaining details of the mission to the Bison Group for the first time. They would coordinate their attacks with the Allied invasion of Italy. "Tomorrow," he told them, "The Navy will provide transportation to Algiers. Once in Algiers, you will switch to a civilian ferry to infiltrate target cities in southern Italy.

Giuseppe interjected, "Signore," he asked politely, "You are sending us to *southern* Italy? Imagine that you sent someone from, let's say, Vermont to infiltrate, say, Alabama? Do you think any of the locals would notice anything? That he talks funny?" Giuseppe continued, "I'm from the Tyrol. Anywhere south of Rome, I'm going to stick out like a sore thumb the minute I open my mouth." He paused, and then continued, "What idiot came up with this hare-brained scheme?"

Then he asked when they were going to be issued their American passports.

Lieutenant Downey replied stiffly that he was under a gross misimpression. The whole point in choosing aliens from Fort Missoula was that they were non-persons. Using Italian natives provided America with plausible deniability. They were being repatriated to Italy. Isn't that what he wanted?

The sound of voices emanating from the Bison Group meeting room grew louder and more agitated.

Giuseppe continued, "Do you think all Italians are stupid? Or just us? A bomb explodes in the train station. Men, women and children are killed and maimed. There's a recently arrived stranger in town. He talks funny. He has no passport. He can't account for his whereabouts for the last three years. Do you think the Carabinieri are going to call Sherlock Holmes to figure this out?"

Giuseppe continued in a somewhat louder voice, "Let's suspend disbelief, and assume that – somehow – after the explosion, I survive a manhunt by the Fascists and the Carabinieri. Your invasion works perfectly, without a hitch. American soldiers pour into town and restore order. I approach the first American soldier I see and tell him, in really shitty English, that I'm really an American secret operative and that he should immediately stop what he's doing and arrange to have me transported back to America. But I have no papers to prove it."

The sound of half a dozen voices from the Bison Group echoes down the hallways.

Lieutenant Downey tries to stem the cacophony. He angrily points out the American taxpayer's expense in transporting and training the Bison Group. Regrettably, Giuseppe was unacquainted with the finer points of the etiquette of addressing officers.

Suddenly a sound like thunder rolling echoes down the glistening corridors. It is the sound of someone pounding on a wooden desk so forcefully that it seems the legs are about to splinter, accompanied by a voice shouting, "Why should I give a shit how much the American taxpayer spent on my incarceration or training? You can take your bison and shove him up your arse."

The din of typewriters in the neighboring offices suddenly peters out like the air escaping from a punctured tire. The deafening silence is shattered once more, by a *voche crescendo*.

"You, *Sir*, are a fucking asshole!" This echoed through the corridors resonating up the stairwells to the third floor and beyond.

The following morning Giuseppe woke up in a jail cell at a place called the Gloucester INS Detention Center in New Jersey just across the Delaware River from Philadelphia. He blinked hard trying to reorient himself in the harsh August sunlight pouring through the small window of his cell. He could discern the buzzing of a fly. It was trapped between the

glass panes, bouncing hysterically back and forth like the ball in a pinball machine shimmying between the bumpers, unable to comprehend why he couldn't escape.

SECRET

Inspector in Charge   7 August 1943

United States immigration Center
Gloucester City, New Jersey

Subject: Return of Paroles

Dear Sir:

Giuseppe Gardellin and Simone Riulina, enemy aliens, are herewith being returned to the Department of Justice.

These men agreed to come into our organization for training and subsequent entry into the Army of the United States. Considerable expense was incurred in bringing them to Washington from Missoula Montana. At the last minute they refused to go through with their promise and we feel that they should be dealt with in a manner most severe.

We would not recommend sending them back to Missoula, Montana, but would favor keeping them separated and under close surveillance.

The background of the subject men is well known to Mr. Otto Gitlin of the Department of Justice, and we would advise that before final disposition is made in this case that he be consulted. Meanwhile, we will discuss this situation with him personally.

Again we emphasize that these men, because of the nature of their feeling toward the United States Government and their subsequent actions, should be given no privileges whatever and never again be allowed to enter the United States of America.

Will you please give to Ensign Harris, in whose custody these men are being returned to you, a release for our organization?

Very truly yours,

William W, Downey

Lieutenant, USNR

SECRET

Mr. Lee Gitlin   20 August 1943
Department of justice
Washington D.C.

Dear Mr. Gitlin:

Confirming our telephone conversation of this date, it is requested that the following named men be closely confined with a minimum of privileges, until the conclusion of the Italian campaign: Riulina, Bruno Simone / Gardellin, Giuseppe / Lepko, Antonio

It is further requested that all communications to and from these men be strictly censored. This request is made in the interest of security and to protect the other alien Italians composing the group to which these men formerly belonged. Although they were not inducted into the U.S. Army, all three of the above named men are in possession of secret information, which, if communicated to outside sources would lead to serious repercussions for all personnel involved as well as for the Office of Strategic Services.

At the conclusion of the Italian campaign, the restrictions mentioned above might be somewhat relaxed, but it is strongly recommended that no parole be granted in these cases.

Very truly yours, Edward Breed

Lieut. Commander, USNR

The original purpose of the Gloucester INS facility was to divert a portion of the immigration traffic from Ellis Island to Philadelphia. Originally a private mansion, it functioned principally as an administrative office. It was never designed to operate as a jail. It was jerry-rigged with enough cells to accommodate 50 inmates for short periods of time, typically a week or two, such as immigrants quarantined for suspected health issues or criminals awaiting deportation. It lacked all the facilities one normally associates with a humane detention facility. There were no classrooms, no infirmary, no gym, no library, no exercise yard and no workshops. There was virtually nothing to occupy an inmate's time. Inmates had access to what had originally been the house garden, a tree lined yard with gravel paths with benches, not unlike a small urban park, except it was surrounded by a fence topped with concertina wire. Giuseppe spent the better part of every day in this yard reading books and newspapers. As he progressed from Dante to Shakespeare the trees on either side of his bench faded from green to yellow. They turned to red as he waded into Melville, then brown by the time of Ahab's blind rage towards the white whale.

He saw pictures in a magazine of children carving jack-o-lanterns. All Soul's Day was just another milestone in the liturgical calendar in Italy. Here they carve orange gourds into grotesque faces and put candles inside. Americans do such bizarre things.

By the time he was floating down the Mississippi with Huckleberry Finn, a cold rain had driven him inside. Grey clouds rolled in and a curtain of fog descended over the yard, so thick that Giuseppe couldn't see the trees at the far edge of the yard. After dinner, laying on his bunk in the dark,

Giuseppe slowly drifted off to sleep. The silence was periodically punctuated by the basso profundo of a fog horn and the bleating reply from a freighter steaming down the Delaware River on the outgoing tide just beyond the fence.

During times of crisis and lacking trustworthy information from either government or news media, rumor and speculation fill the void and become the medium of exchange. Now that Giuseppe's letters had inexplicably ceased the rumor mill went into overdrive. Giuseppe's family wrote desperate letters to Ettorre imploring for news about Giuseppe. Ettorrie's reply looked like lacework; the censer's razor had devoured it like a hyena stripping a carcass to a bare skeleton.

Despite efforts by the INS and OSS to staunch the flow, a minute fragment of information filtered back to Cittadella. Ettorre wrote a long rambling letter, prattling about the weather, and what they ate for lunch, and the new shoes that he had been issued. Interspersed in all of this was a disjointed parody of Aesop's fable where he wrote that he and the other ants in the Idaho lumber camp were diligently husbanding wood for the winter while a certain, unnamed cricket was playing the fiddle in the linen fields in Gloucester. Back in Italy, his wife put two and two together and got the message.

In response to this minute scrap of information, Giuseppe's sister Giovanella decided to reach out to her friend in America, Mrs Scringi, initiating a serpentine chain of communication that would have more twists and turns than the Haymaker's Jig.

7

THE SALOONKEEPER'S TALE

In the 1880's anthracite coal was discovered north of Mauch Chunk, Pennsylvania. The mine owners needed experienced miners and the premier hard rock miners in the world were in the Tyrol boring tunnels through the Alps. They sent recruiters with a simple offer: A one-way ticket and a job in what was arguably the most dangerous occupation in America.

No unemployment insurance, no disability insurance, no social security and no food stamps, but you got to keep every penny you earned. There was no income tax and no mandatory tithe.

You could go wherever you pleased. You didn't have to ask a landlord or party apparatchik for permission to change occupations or move to a different town.

Thousands of immigrants thought that this was a good deal. They arrived on Ellis Island from the Tyrol, Ireland and Poland with a note pinned to their jacket that read, in English, "Put me on the train to Philadelphia. Transfer to Hazleton."

Fortunato Bones was among those Tyrolean immigrants. Born in the late 1800's in Bolzano, 150 kilometers west of Cittadella, he immigrated to America with his family as a small child.

By the time he was ten, he was working as a breaker boy in the coal mines near Sheppton just outside Hazleton. In his mid thirties he was diagnosed with black lung disease. The doctor calmly reported that he might live a year, maybe two, assuming he continued working in the mine. His wife determined that he would find a living outside of the mines. She knew a fellow Tyrolean immigrant "with money to lend". She borrowed the money and bought the Sheppton Saloon, expanded it to include a boarding house and a shanty and she and her husband ran the business together. The venture bought him a decade of life. After he died, Nona Bones continued running the business with her daughter, Fiora Falk. With Nona's passing, Fiora succeeded to the throne, becoming queen-bee of the Sheppton Saloon.

The Sheppton Saloon served as the bar, dining room, banquet hall, union hall, news room and unofficial bank, presided over by Fiora Falk, den mother and hardnosed businesswoman, who knew everyone's business and was as discrete as a priest.

When immigrants arrived in Sheppton, Fiora Falk's Saloon was their first stop. New arrivals found familiar food, decent lodging and short term credit until arrangements could be made for living quarters in a company house and credit established at the company store. Among those new arrivals in 1938 were Giovanella's friends, Mr and Mrs. Scringi. Mrs. Scringi and Fiora became best friends, a connection that lasted the rest of their lives.

Then, in the autumn of 1943 Mrs. Scringi received a letter from Giovanella in Cittadella that had her distraught to tears. Giuseppe's sister, Giovanella, wrote to Mrs. Scringi telling her that Giuseppe was incarcerated in a place called "Gloucester", imploring her to visit Giuseppe, find out the reason for the secrecy surrounding his incarceration and see firsthand his treatment and condition. Giovanella didn't realize the distance between Sheppton and Gloucester and was unaware that, without access to an automobile, such a trip was virtually impossible for Mrs. Scringi.

Mrs. Scringi turned to her best friend for help. When Fiora heard her friend's dilemma, she smiled and hugged her girlfriend and told her not to worry, it would be taken care of.

Fiora told Mrs. Scringi that her sister and brother-in-law, DioMira and John Tamea, had recently moved from Sheppton to Philadelphia, just across the river from Gloucester. She would write to them that night as soon as she closed the bar. She would tell them about Giuseppe. She assured Mrs. Scringi that her brother-in-law was a canny, determined man who would find a way to contact Giuseppe. Giuseppe would soon have a visitor they could trust.

When Fiora reached out to her sister and brother-in-law, John wrote back and agreed to contact the missing crewman.

8

THE COAL MINER'S TALE

The same tide of immigrants that swept Fortunato Bones to the American anthracite fields of Pennsylvania carried another family from the Tyrol. Like Fortunato, John Tamea emigrated with his family as a small child. They settled in Sheppton on the outskirts of Hazleton, one of the largest Tyrolean conclaves in America.

Above: Breaker Boys picking slate.

Below: Trap-door boys

John Tamea was pulled from school after third grade to work in the coal mines as a breaker boy picking slate, then a trap man, opening and closing trap doors for the mules. The doors had to be kept closed so the ventilation system could exhaust potentially explosive coal dust and methane gas from the deep mine shafts. He worked as a mule driver, shovel man, pick man, driller and blaster. In those days miners worked 10 to 12 hours a day in crevasses as small as 30 inches, knocking coal loose with a hand pick and shoveling it into a mule cart. Coal doesn't fall out of the vein in nice little briquettes like you buy in the supermarket for the grill; it breaks loose in chunks the size of bowling balls; the breaker reduces it to bite sized pieces. The shovel man has to scoop these chunks into the coal car which was pulled by a mule to the scale house. It was piece work, paid by the ton. The pick man and shovel man split the tonnage pay.

John Tamea and DioMira Bones met as children in grade school. They remained friends growing up. In their twenties, they fell in love and married. They had four children over the intervening years.

The Tamea family:

(Clockwise from left) DioMira (seated), Charlotte (standing on chair with her mother), John (standing in rear), Conrad (Standing in front of his father), and Violet (seated on small chair). Jackie would follow ten years after this photograph was taken.

John and DioMira lived in a company house. They bought their groceries, clothes and the carbide for John's miner's lamp at the company store. They wanted a better life for their children; they made sure their children graduated from High School.

John Tamea was not a warm fuzzy guy. He had his share of bar room brawls, labor disputes and close scrapes with the law. But John Tamea was a man you could count on. If you were a shovel or pick man you wanted John for your partner. He worked as hard as the mules that pulled the coal cars. When there was a cave-in, he burrowed with the tenacity of a ground hog until he saved the trapped men or retrieved the bodies.

He loaned money he didn't have and time he couldn't spare to help a neighbor repair his house or his car. Every winter he butchered his deer. Every autumn he made sausage but hated having to kill the pig. One Easter he made the mistake of buying a pair of live lambs early and keeping them too long in the yard. Before it was time to slaughter them, the children had named them. They wound up hale and hearty back on the farm.

9

THE

TELEPHONE OPERATOR'S TALE

Eight year old Charlotte woke up in her bedroom in the house in Sheppton, a diffused morning light filling the room. Her older sister Violet was asleep in the opposite bed. Charlotte bounced out of bed, bounded across the narrow room and shook her sister awake.

"Wake UP! Wake UP sleepy head! It's Sunday." Violet turned and looked at her. "Wake up! It's Sunday but we don't have to go to church today. Remember? We pick blueberries today."

When the girls went down stairs to the kitchen, their mother was already standing at the stove. Their father was seated at the table nursing a cup of coffee.

"Hurry girls. The eggs will be ready in a few minutes."

Even though it was early, the day was already warm enough that the girls ran out the back door to the outhouse in bare feet and nightgowns.

"Run upstairs and get dressed."

"And get your brother up. He has to go today, too."

By the time DioMira was clearing plates from the table, Shilio's truck was idling in front of the house. DioMira and John crowded into the cab next to Shilio while the children scrambled into the cargo bed.

The truck traveled only a few miles until the road began to rise and the truck was climbing through a cool green tunnel of pine trees and rhododendron shrubs. The truck crested a bald headed mountain; Charlotte could see across a fluorescent green velvet valley, row after row of indigo toped mountains stretching into the July haze like petrified waves on the ocean. Shilio downshifted and let the engine ease the truck down a long curving decent, pulling off the road at a firebreak near the valley bottom. After they disembarked from the truck, everyone put on a leather belt fitted with a basket attached to the front. Everyone that is, except for Conrad, who carried a stack of wooden flats loaded with empty one-pint splint boxes. Grey granite boulders littered the firebreak like a herd of elephants marching through a forest of ferns. The family marched single file along the path weaving between the boulders and through the ferns down a gentle slope towards a small stream. Near the stream the ground was moist and spongy. A stand of blueberry shrubs stretched from one end of the firebreak to the other. As the family harvested the plump, pregnant berries, Charlotte stayed close to her father, peppering him with questions and chatting through the whole morning. Each time they filled the basket on their belt they would empty it into the pint boxes in the wooden flats; when a flat was filled Conrad carried it back up the hill to the truck, bringing an empty flat back in its place.

At mid day they spread a quilt over the ground; they could smell the crushed ferns under the blanket. There was lunch of Tyrolean salami called 'lughanighe', cheese, and bread that DioMira baked the day before. There was a bottle of red wine for John, DioMira and Shilio, and a bucket with ice and soda pop for the children – a rare treat.

When the last flats were loaded, the family hiked back to the truck for the ride home. When DioMira and the children arrived home they took out four pints of berries for pies. John and Shilio drove the rest to the wholesaler. During the depression, the location of a mother lode of berries remained a closely guarded secret confined to immediate family. In recounting the experience seventy years later, Charlotte was noticeably vague about the precise location.

Oldest daughter Violet was the pioneer and artist of the family. A gifted violinist, when she graduated from high school she moved to Philadelphia to study music at a conservatory. She quickly realized that neither she nor her family had the financial resources to complete a classical music education. With a pragmatism born of necessity she enrolled in a vocational technical school and in a few months was working as a beautician. She soon had a job and her own apartment in center city Philadelphia.

When Charlotte graduated from high school, like her sister Violet, she too left this town perched in the Pocono Mountains of Pennsylvania, returning only for occasional visits to older relatives.

Charlotte's senior trip was to New York City. When it was time to board the bus for the trip home to Sheppton, Charlotte, who had a predilection to be impulsive, bolted from the group and boarded a bus to Philadelphia instead. The bus rolled across the flat crazy-quilt of vegetable farms separating the concrete islands of New York and Philadelphia. She was buffeted by the warm June air blowing in the open windows. She thought about her room in the house in Sheppton. She thought about her mother making dinner right then on the coal stove in the kitchen. She was already home sick, but what was there to do in Sheppton? Jobs for men were scarce enough; a job for a young woman was virtually unthinkable. She loved her father and mother but there had to be more to life than marrying a coal miner.

Violet was shocked when she answered a knock on the door of her apartment and saw her sister standing there, having had no advanced warning. After a few seconds to sort out the new arrangement of things the realization dawned on her that she had just acquired an instant roommate. She greeted her sister with an odd mixture of approbation and reprimand.

That night as Charlotte lay on the sofa, her temporary bed, she gradually acclimated herself to the novel night sounds that filtered in through the open windows as she sank in to a deep sleep: honking auto horns, the wailing of a distant siren dying off in the distance, music from a radio somewhere, the faint rumble of a distant trolley car, and she knew with certainty that she had made the right decision.

At breakfast the next morning, Violet tacitly pointed out that Charlotte's half of the rent was due on the first of the month, two weeks distant. She helped Charlotte vet the 'Help Wanted' ads, highlighting ones within walking distance of public transportation. By her second day in Philadelphia, Charlotte was waitressing at a White Castle burger restaurant.

Sanguine about waitressing, she continued looking for something better.

The same technology destroying traditional craft trades in Europe was simultaneously creating new opportunities for American women previously confined solely to the role of housewives. The new technology came in the form of the telephone. Initially confined to large businesses and government facilities, it gradually expanded into professional offices like doctors and lawyers.

As prices came down they permeated to grocery stores and the corner drug store and even gained a foothold in select private residences.

Switchboard operators were originally teenage boys who were agile enough to master the plug and cord chorography, but tended to be obstreperous when dealing with customers. Seeking to project an image of polite, pleasant customer service, AT&T jettisoned the teenage boys and deliberately mandated that the job of 'switchboard operator' be an almost exclusive female domain. By her first September in Philadelphia, Charlotte secured one of these coveted high tech job with Bell Telephone as a cord-and-plug switchboard operator.

***

Just like the oil cartels today, in the 1930's coal producers adjusted output to prop up the price. They worked overtime when snow and freezing temperatures blanketed the country and stockpiles were low and cut back production during the summer when stockpiles were high.

The miners were used to temporary layoffs. But by the mid 1930's layoffs become more frequent and protracted as the coal veins started petering out. The ranks of idle miners swelled until company stores cut off credit. Younger miners were the first to leave, drifting away to coal mines in Montana, taconite mines in Michigan, silver mines in Colorado. Many went to New York City where they dug the Lincoln Tunnel and the subway tubes. In Sheppton and other towns in the Pocono Mountains, entire blocks of company houses sat empty.

Those that stayed behind turned to bootleg mining, also known as "Robbing the Pillars".

***

John, Conrad and Frank were up well before sunrise. When Shilio pulled his truck up in front of the house the men crowded into the cramped cab and the truck lurched out into a light snow fall just as daylight was beginning to break. There weren't any tire tracks in the snow, even on the main road through town. They drove a few miles out of town past the front gate of one of the mining operations. The gates were chained shut. The guard house was empty. A large sign with the mine name stood next to the gate. The bolts on one of the legs had rusted away and the sign clanged haplessly against the useless leg in the stiff breeze.

They drove about a mile and a half past the main entrance to an all but unnoticeable gap in the trees on the right side of the road. Shilio turned the truck into this gap and drove a few hundred yards through pine trees on a double track so narrow the tree branches were squeaking against the sides of the truck. The truck emerged into a large meadow. Fresh snow and brittle frozen grass crunched under the tires as he drove across the meadow. The truck stopped. The men got out of the truck and milled about like chickens scratching for grub until they found what they were looking for, a narrow hole a couple feet across; the ventilation shaft of an abandoned mine hundreds of feet below. The men dragged three wooden beams out from the truck bed. The beams were from an abandoned barn; ten inches square by twenty five feet long. They assembled the beams into a tripod over the hole and hung a pulley from the peak of the tripod. They fished a rope through the pulley and tied one end of the rope to eye hooks that Shilio had welded to the rim of a 55 gallon drum; they tied the other end to the front bumper of Shilio's truck. John, Conrad and Frank donned their hard hats and squeezed together into the drum while Shilio climbed into the cab of the truck. He put the truck in gear and drove slowly towards the tripod, lowering the three men into the pitch black of the mine shaft. After what seemed like an awfully long time the drum with the men inside thumped rudely onto the floor of the mine. The men climbed out, lit the carbide lamps on their helmets and set to work.

When coal is dug from the ground, you can't get it all. Columns ranging from room size to house size have to be left to support the roof. Bootleg miners nibble away at these supports, hence the term "robbing the pillars".

The men drilled holes into the sides of the pillars. With no steam or electricity available, it had to be done by hand, one man striking the drill with a sledge hammer while the other twisted it with a wrench. They set dynamite into the holes, walked a few hundred feet away and set off the charge. Then the fractured coal had to be pick axed out and hauled to the makeshift elevator in a wheelbarrow. It was shoveled from the wheelbarrow into the fifty five gallon drum. Shilio would drive the truck in reverse pulling the drum to the surface then tipping it. In a typical week they could extract enough coal to fill the truck one time. Shilio drove the coal to Philadelphia to sell.

When John's son Conrad finished high school he stayed in Sheppton working in Shilio's welding shop. He became an adept machinist and welder, doing maintenance and repair work on coal breakers and mining machinery at the dwindling mining companies still operating. The work was sporadic and paid little. He supplemented his income working with his father and Uncle Frank scavenging coal. One day the three of them were working underground with pickaxes when they heard a cracking sound like a close rifle shot. A hail storm of coal and pebbles began raining down from the roof. The men dashed towards the makeshift elevator. Not waiting for Shilio to haul the bucket they scrambled up the rope, popping out at the surface like startled prairie dogs. As they emerged from the hole, John and Frank bent over alternately coughing and laughing, covered with black soot and spitting out coal dust. Conrad was less amused, yanking off his hardhat, throwing it on the frozen ground yelling, "Jesus Christ. There has to be a better way to make a living than this shit."

Two days later Conrad joined the Civilian Conservation Corps.

A few weeks later he was gone. He wrote to his family often. In one of his letters is a photograph of him with his crew in the Rocky Mountains working on the National Park trails. There is a huge canyon in the background. He looks very happy.

A few months later, John and Frank were at the sitting on the running board of Shilio's truck next to the abandoned mine eating lunch. Frank asked his brother, "Well, are you ready to get back to work or are you going to sit here all day admiring the view?" He was surprised by his brother's answer.

John replied calmly, "Piss on it. Conrad's right. I'm not going down that fucking hole one more time. There has to be something better."

By that summer factory jobs were sputtering to life in major cities throughout the country. John Tamea threw in the sponge on mining and followed Violet and Charlotte to Philadelphia. He found a job on the assembly line at the Budd Rail Car Company.

This new job contrasted favorably with mining; wages were better, you worked standing up and there was a much reduced likelihood of being killed or maimed in a cave-in or explosion. John and DioMira purchased a house at 3540 North 15th street in Philadelphia. Violet and Charlotte gave up their apartment and moved in with their parents. Frank followed a few months later.

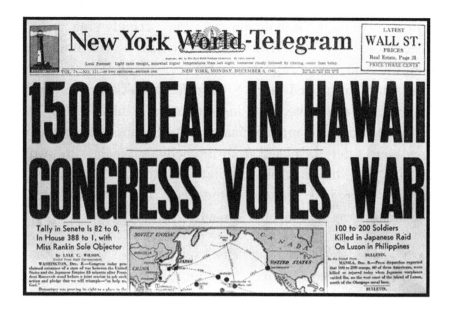

Switchboard operators worked most weekends, their days off rotated through the week. For Charlotte, Sunday, December-7-1941 was an ordinary workday. Violet was home doing housework, listening to Sammy Kaye and the Kaydettes on the radio. At 2:29 in the afternoon the program was interrupted by a news bulletin. Japan attacked a naval base in Hawaii. Details were sketchy. No one knew how serious it was. When Charlotte arrived home at the end of her shift Violet told her about the news bulletins punctuating the afternoon radio programming.

During her Monday commute to work, the mood on the trolley and subway was unusually subdued. By the time of President Franklin Roosevelt's radio address Monday evening, America was beginning to grasp the extent of the carnage.

It made no sense. Americans were aware of the war in Europe, but couldn't understand why Europe was embarking on a program of self immolation for the second time in a generation. To Americans, the Fascist - Communist confrontation was a tug of war between political ideologies that both constituted insane extrema. Now America was inexplicably confronted by a Japan apparently inhabited by 70 million insatiable homicidal maniacs. Americans had assumed they were safely insulated from the bellicose bedlam by two oceans, an illusion that Admiral Yamamoto shattered in slightly over two hours. Within days the United States declared war against Japan, Germany, and Italy.

Two years later, just after Thanksgiving 1943 Zia Fiora's letter arrived. John read and reread Fiora's letter, trying to sort out in his own mind the scant details and the tangled connections between Fiora and Mrs Scringi, and Mrs Scringi's friend Giovanella in Italy whose brother had suddenly vanished in a place called Gloucester. It never occurred to him not to help a fellow Tyrolean.

Though not well educated, John was not stupid. Years of working in hazardous conditions in the mines taught him to think things through in advance. Some of the men he worked with lived around Gloucester. He made discrete enquiries, gleaning as much detail as possible. They were familiar with the INS building; a prominent feature in Gloucester right on the waterfront.

Faced with the challenge of penetrating a secret jail, the germ of an idea slowly came in to focus. Charlotte was blossoming into a beautiful young woman. Six foot tall, athletic, blond, with blue eyes and a radiant smile, she was outgoing and engaging with a striking innocence about her. Although she couldn't afford jewelry or costly accessories, Charlotte patterned her choice of clothes after the secretaries who worked in the executive suite; invariably wearing hat and gloves. John knew instinctively that she was perfect for the assignment. But she should have someone to go with her. John conferred with his brother Frank whose daughter Lillian was Charlotte's best friend.

Charlotte and Lillian were ambivalent about the whole affair. Charlotte had worked on Thanksgiving the week prior. A Saturday off from work was a rare chance to meet with her friends. They had plans for the day and were baffled as to why their fathers cared about some stranger from the old country anyway. They were unconvinced by the terse "Because he's a Tyrolean." Through an adroitly negotiated combination of parental authority, assurances they would be back in time to join their friends later in the afternoon, and money for lunch at a restaurant, the girls reluctantly acquiesced.

John jotted down instructions concerning the trolley route and ferry connection. Intelligence on the person they were supposed to meet was nebulous at best; they had little beyond a name and the name of the town of his origin. John was intentionally vague on what they should do when they arrived, confident the girls could improvise once they got there.

It was a brisk Saturday in December when Charlotte and Lillian set out on their bizarre mission. As they stood leaning on the deck rail of the ferry, a sun lit Philadelphia skyline glided by slowly in the background. Charlotte buttoned her coat up to the neck against the cold as they speculated about the person they would soon meet.

Lillian asked in an exasperated voice, "Why are you such a sour puss this morning?"

"Why not?" replied Charlotte. "I can't believe I let Daddy talk us into this, wasting our whole day on this stupid wild goose chase."

"What do you think this guy is like, anyway?" asked Lillian.

"With a name like 'Giuseppe'? Remember the guys from the old country we saw getting off the train in Sheppton and walking up the street to Fiora's saloon their first day in America? All the same; the suit like a dog's bed, a cheap cardboard suitcase, handlebar moustache, teeth missing, smelling like salami and too much Brilliantine in their hair."

"Do you suppose he speaks English?"

"Well if not, we're going to get plenty of practice speaking Tyrolean."

Simple plans work best.

Charlotte and Lillian walked in the front door at the Gloucester INS Detention Center and politely asked the guard if they could please see – after checking John's note - one "Giuseppe Gardellin". The guard was incredulous. None of the Italian detainees had ever had a visitor.

He asked them to wait a few minutes while he conferred with one of the other guards, who picked up a telephone and called someone. They overheard the man on the telephone, "…couple of girls. Look about sixteen, seventeen tops."

After the guard hung up the receiver, he informed them that they could visit for 60 minutes. They had to speak English. Don't touch the prisoner. Don't give anything to the prisoner, not even a pencil or paper. They must not give the prisoner money.

Giuseppe was reading quietly in his cell when the guard told him that he had visitors. He was incredulous. A visitor? He initially dismissed it as a practical joke. The closest person he know in America was in Montana. When the guard insisted that he really did have visitors, he figured he had nothing to lose to investigate.

As Charlotte and Lillian stood waiting in the Visitor's Room, a young man emerged from a door at the other end of the room. Everything about his appearance was sharp; tanned and muscular, pants with sharp creases, crisp white shirt and burnished brown dress shoes. He entered the room with such an air of authority that for a split second they thought he was the head warden, but quickly realized he was too young to be even be a guard much less a warden.

Charlotte leaned over and whispered behind her hand in her cousin's ear, "Now if we were here to meet someone like that, that would be different".

The young man looked about, strode up to the girls and greeted them, smiling broadly "Buon giorno. I am Giuseppe Gardellin. It is my pleasure to meet you."

A pregnant silence ensued for several seconds; Charlotte and Lillian looked at Giuseppe, wordless. The girls turned and looked at each other wide eyed; each clapped a hand over her mouth trying to suppress laughter. They looked back at Giuseppe, who didn't get the joke but was nonetheless amused. He couldn't imagine where these girls had come from, or how they knew Giovanella, but any day where beautiful women fall out of the sky into your life is a pretty good day.

The meeting started with awkward introductions; the girls explained the circuitous chain of circumstances that had brought them there. Giuseppe vaguely remembered his sister's friend, Mrs. Scringi. They told him that his family wanted him to know that they loved him and were worried about him. As they sat facing each other, Charlotte's hands fluttered back and forth between her lap and her hair like nervous birds. She blushed pink as rose petals each time he looked at her to say something. She turned her head slightly and looked at him from the corners of her eyes. She punctuated her sentences with little nervous bites of her lower lip. Forgetting the prohibition, she gently touched his arm while she was talking to him. The guard pretended not to notice. Most of all they talked.

Sixty minutes felt like sixty seconds.

The girls promised to let his family know he was in good health and spirits. As they prepared to leave, Giuseppe said he would write to them. He asked for their addresses. Charlotte started to fumble in her purse for a pen. He assured them he didn't need to write it down. He would remember.

After a formal and carefully monitored farewell, they left.

On the way home, the girls stopped at the Horn and Hardart restaurant on Market Street. Over coffee Lillian teased her, "Well, he sure wasn't what we expected, was he? What an embarrassing spectacle! You didn't even know I was there. You were blushing every time he looked at you. The two of you making lovey-dovey eyes at each other. I was ready to tell you to get a room."

Charlotte protested that he asked for both their addresses.

"He was being polite. He didn't take his eyes off you the whole time. Che lughanighe; you don't think he's really going to remember our addresses, do you?"

Charlotte was uncharacteristically quiet at dinner that evening. Her parents queried her about the man at the detention center. Charlotte acted blasé and nonchalant about the whole affair, providing only sketchy details. Her parents were exasperated by the lack of any coherent report on the crewman's condition to relay to Mrs. Scringi, other than to say that he was in good health and had received visitors as promised.

Later that night in their bedroom, Charlotte and Violet faced each other propped on one elbow on their beds. The moonlight flowing in under the bottom of the shades cast a pale rectangle on the linoleum floor. They chatted in hushed voices about the handsome young man with the charming accent. Violet said to her, "Let's see if I've got this right? You're head over heels in love with someone you just met today and spoke to for less than an hour? Who barely speaks English? He's officially classified a dangerous alien? He's in jail indefinitely, with no bail, no probation, and no trial scheduled and you can't go on a date? You can't even have a conversation with him without a guard in the room. And he didn't write down your address?"

Violet moaned, "Dearest sister, why do I not see a happy ending to this story?"

L'amore e una cagna. True love never runs smooth.

A week later when Charlotte arrived home from work her mother told her that she had a letter in the mail. The envelope was addressed in neat block printing, postmarked Gloucester, New Jersey and was stamped with the censor's examination mark. Charlotte acted disinterested. She didn't open it, but she dropped it nonchalantly into her purse for later perusal. Only a few lines had been excised by the censor's razor. Her mood was noticeably elevated for several days.

Charlotte spent the following week composing a reply, writing, re-writing, crossing out, discarding, and writing over, until she felt that she had all the ingredients perfectly blended and it tasted just right to her. That improbable letter with the memorized address initiated a chain of correspondence that would float back and forth for the next several years like the shuttlecock in a languorous game of badminton.

Switch boards operated seven days a week. The operator's day off was on a rotating schedule. Two weeks after the letter arrived, Charlotte's day off was a weekday, which facilitated timing her departure when everyone else in the family was out. She retraced the trip to the Gloucester INS Detention Center, with significant changes from her prior visit. This trip was preceded by a visit to the hair salon. She bought a new dress. And, oh, it slipped her mind to tell anyone where she was going.

And she traveled alone this time, having jettisoned her dear cousin, as a girl will do in such circumstances.

Momma wasn't fooled, of course, but decided to wait-and-see for the time being.

In late December, Giuseppe was pleasantly shocked by an unexpected surprise: Christmas cards, two of them, one from Charlotte and one from Father Menninger. The beautiful girl who had fallen out of the sky had replied to his letter. He was equally surprised that Father Jim Menninger from Montana remembered him.

Giuseppe greeted the new year of 1944 with mixed feelings. His new pen pal visitor provided a welcome illumination to his life. If he had to spend a third Christmas in prison, at least Charlotte's letters describing their Christmas made him feel some sense of participating in the holiday. On the other hand, his incarceration appeared interminable. He had spent countless hours over the last four months writing to this office and that office and he knew he was getting the official government sanctioned run around. The military induction office in Washington D.C. replied that in order to volunteer for military service he had to appear in person at the draft office nearest his official address, in Ft Missoula Montana. The Ft Missoula office replied that as a detained alien prisoner he wasn't an official Montana resident and didn't qualify to apply there, and so on. Giuseppe knew that he was a dead letter himself.

What he didn't know was that in the rectory at St Ignatius Montana, Father Menninger was waging an unrelenting charm offensive on his behalf. Every evening he was in his study pounding away on the Underwood typewriter full tilt, reaching out to anyone with influence that he could track down. And Father Menninger tracked down a lot of influential people. In a contest between one Jesuit priest and the United States Government, smart money is on the Jesuit.

After months of steady pressure, a fissure appeared in the rock. By Easter, a letter from the OSS to the Department of Justice inexplicably reversed their former assertion that Giuseppe should be incarcerated indefinitely.

A few weeks after Easter, Giuseppe was transferred from Gloucester to the Ellis Island Detention facility, automatically granting him official New York City resident status. His legal address was now "Room-17, Ellis Island, New York, NY." Now he could apply for military service and US citizenship at the Manhattan Draft Office.

Giuseppe had a one month interim between his release from prison and his induction date. He rented a room on LeRoy Street in lower Manhattan near 14th Street, just northwest of New York's Little Italy neighborhood. He landed a temp agency job with a security company as a night watchman, an ironic position for a dangerous alien. For the first time in five years he was free to walk where ever he pleased without being accompanied by a guard. Giuseppe never said anything about this brief interlude, despite the dramatic change in his circumstances. One can only speculate how he passed the time.

While Charlotte wondered if the yong sailor from the Comte Biancamano was *ever* going to extricate himself from the INS bureaucracy and if she was ever going to see him again, the war came closer to home. Her brother Conrad in the Army Air Corps was assigned as a tail gunner on a B-24 'Liberator' flying bombing missions over Europe. His primary target was the Ploesti oil refineries, which the Germans defended with particular ferocity. Each flight crewman was issued an official logbook. At the completion of each mission, the commander recorded his participation in the mission and signed and stamped his log. When a crewman completed 35 missions he was rotated to a non-flight assignment. The odds of flying 35 missions without being killed or captured were a 30 percent *survival* rate. Over two thirds of the aviators who flew missions over Ploesti were lost. Charlotte, along with her mother and sisters, did a lot of praying. Conrad Tamea is in the back row. At 6-foot-3 and the tallest member of the flight crew, he's easy to spot.

10

The Soldier's Tale

After his hiatus at the Ellis Island Prison, the OSS pushed the paperwork through channels and Giuseppe was inducted into the US Military. On his last day in New York, before reporting for duty, at a courthouse in Manhattan, Giuseppe raised his right hand and swore,

"I hereby declare, on oath that I absolutely and entirely renounce and abjure all allegiance and fidelity to any foreign prince, potentate, state, or sovereignty of whom or which I have heretofore been a subject or citizen; that I will support and defend the Constitution and laws of the United States of America against all enemies, foreign and domestic; that I will bear true faith and allegiance to the same; that I will bear arms on behalf of the United States when required by the law; that I will perform noncombatant service in the Armed Forces of the United States when required by the law; that I will perform work of national importance under civilian direction when required by the law; and that I take this obligation freely without any mental reservation or purpose of evasion; so help me God."

Giuseppe had achieved the previously unimaginable; he was an American.

An experienced seaman, Giuseppe naturally applied for induction into the US Navy. After reviewing the background of someone who had never driven so much as a motor scooter, the US military, in their infinite wisdom, deduced that Giuseppe was ideal candidate for the tank corp. They were right. He fit hand-in-glove with the rough and tumble tankers of Patton's 4th Armored Division with the same ease that he fit in with the ranchers and lumberjacks in Idaho.

There he befriended Paul Dick, a man his own age who grew up on the streets of New York and who spoke with the most eloquent Bronx accent you ever heard. Their friendship lasted a life time.

Giuseppe and Paul were assigned to the 37th Armor Regiment led by Colonel Creighton Abrams. The colonel later rose to command all US forces in Viet Nam and served as US Army Chief of Staff in the 1970's. He is the namesake of the Abrams tank. The 37th Armor Regiment was assigned to the 4th Armored Division headed by Major General John S. Wood.

Most of Giuseppe's fellow soldiers were further from home than they had ever been in their lives; they felt surrounded by alien people who spoke unintelligible languages and they chaffed under their newly imposed military regimen. Giuseppe was closer to home than he had been in six years. For Giuseppe it was refreshing to hear familiar languages for the first time in years. After years of incarceration, Giuseppe was exhilarated by his new found freedom. Little wonder he emerged as unofficial leader. Years later Paul recounted, "Giuseppe was a cross between Geronimo and a cicada wasp, a natural born warrior who knew instinctively what the enemy was going to do before he knew it himself. In that split second between thought and action, Giuseppe struck unhesitatingly with deadly speed and decisiveness. When we were under fire, we could hear the officers over the walkie-talkie but we kept our eyes on Giuseppe and followed his lead. We were all scared shitless, but Giuseppe always seemed to know just what to do and never revealed a moment's hesitation or fear."

The 37th did not participate in the D-Day landing on June 6, 1944. Shortly after, on July 28, the 4th Armored Division attacked through the infantry lines and began its historic race across France.

In a quick attack on August 31, during a driving rainstorm, the 37th captured the bridge across the Meuse river at Commercy before the Germans could blow it up. The 37th proceeded to advance 700 miles in seven weeks, crossing three major rivers, and was within 70 miles of the German border.

From September 19 through 22, the Germans tried to push the 37th back across the Moselle River. At Moyenvic, the 37th saw one of the largest tank-to-tank engagements of the war, losing 14 Shermans while knocking out 55 Panthers and Tigers during the Germans' unsuccessful counter attack.

On September 22, the 37th's M4 tanks swept south through Coincourt and Bures to the Rhine-Marne Canal. Counterattack followed counterattack as the desperate Wehrmacht tried to dislodge the 3rd Army from its position, but as the toll of Panthers mounted the attacks dwindled and finally ceased. For its tenacity in the Moselle River valley, the 37th was awarded a Croix de Guerre with Palm by a grateful French government, its second such award, the initial honor in Normandy.

On November 11, the 37th was caught on the road and suffered heavy casualties because they could not maneuver off-road due to the bottomless mud.

The Shermans of Company-A were the first 4th Armored vehicles to enter Germany near Rimling on December 16. On the same day that Company-A entered the Reich, Hitler played his last trump north of where Giuseppe and Paul were resting from five months in action. The German 5th Panzer Army spearheaded the attack that opened the **Battle of the Bulge**.

The 37th received orders to march north against the German penetration on December 18, 1944. On the same day the 101st Airborne Division was moved by truck to establish a strongpoint at the key road and rail junction of **Bastogne**, in Belgium. By the time the 37th arrived at the south flank of the German position, the 101st was cut off on all sides by the enemy drive. The 37th became the point of the 4th Armored Division's drive to relieve the paratroopers in Bastogne.

Three days before Christmas, Giuseppe and Paul were up early and by 6 AM the tankers of the 37th had moved out in a feathery snowfall attacking northward against German airborne troops.

That Christmas morning, Giuseppe and his fellow tankers jumped off from Bercheaux and swiftly took Bauxles-Rosieres, Nives, and Remoiville. At dawn December 26, 1944, the 37th struck again taking Remichampagne.

Two towns lay between the 37th and Bastogne, Clochimont and Assenois, both heavily defended by German troops.

Beyond Assenois was a heavy wooded area concealing blockhouses that lined the road to Bastogne. Abrams ordered, "Put the Shermans i high gear and barge through the defenses, stopping for nothing and leaving mopping up to the companies following". By 16:45 Lt. Boggess of the 37th shook hands with 2nd Lt. Webster of the 326th Engineers, 101st Airborne Division.

For their relief of Bastogne the 37th was awarded the Presidential Unit Citation that members still wear today.

Days later Giuseppe and Paul had a brief respite as the mess truck and mail caught up to them. A near-freezing rain turned the belated Christmas dinner of turkey and mashed potatoes into a soupy mush in the tin mess kit plates. The mail brought Giuseppe a long letter from Charlotte filled with Christmas greetings, worry, love and prayers, turning the cold mush into a holiday banquet. Charlotte described the Christmas tree in the parlor, the decorations in the department stores on Market

Street, the Christmas Eve dinner, and what she was doing with her friends for the holidays. Reading a letter from your girlfriend is like sitting next to a warm hearth on a cold night.

On March 25, 1945, the 5th Infantry Division crossed the Rhine in landing craft near Oppenheim. A pontoon bridge was quickly constructed and by the 26th of March, the 37th was across along with the rest of the 4th Armored Division.

The Frankfurt-Berlin Autobahn was the 4th Armored Division's axis of advance. In contrast to official news photographs showing tank columns as models of military order and decorum, Giuseppe and Paul's stories painted a starkly contrasting picture, describing tanks festooned with clanging cooking utensils, drying laundry, salami, cheese, mattresses and beer kegs liberated from local breweries.

Officers squinted at these departures from military protocol so long as the tankers continued their unflinching assault on the Nazi Wehrmacht.

By April, 1945 the 37th had driven deep into central Germany, at which point Hitler was conscripting anyone who could carry a gun. Giuseppe was shocked to discover bazooka emplacements and machine gun nests "manned" by boys barely old enough to be in high school and old men well past retirement.

Giuseppe described the symbiosis between the tanks and the infantry at this stage of the war. The tanks protected the infantry from machine gun fire. In turn, infantry enforced a draconian calculus on the Germans: A bazooka might take out a tank but, hit or miss, they invariably made sure the bazooka man paid for the shot with his life.

On April 4, 1945, the 4th Armored Division overran Ohrduf, a sub camp of the Buchenwald Concentration Camp. Word came back up the line from the lead soldiers entering the camp: Send medics and a translator. Giuseppe was sent in with the medics. They were among the first Allied soldiers to enter the camp.

Words fail. None of the first-hand eyewitnesses has ever been able to describe the visceral reaction of liberating these camps. The thing that came to Giuseppe's mind when he first beheld the emaciated prisoners and corpses stacked like cordwood was his trip to Germany all those years ago to see the Fuehrer. He recalled the parades and pageantry, the speeches, the sea of waving flags and throngs of cheering people who wanted so desperately to believe this was the dawn of a new government that would bring stable currency, steady employment and security to their homeland. Giuseppe's life lesson, one that he reiterated frequently though his life: A sea of waving flags is invariably the harbinger of an impending load of horse shit.

Giuseppe tried to explain what he saw in a letter to his father, but it never quite came out right. He tried to explain it in his letters to his brother the priest. Years later he tried to explain it to his son. He would start out, but after a few sentences his voice would trail off and all he could say was that, despite knowing five languages, there were no words, in Italian or English or Spanish, or any language that he knew that could describe it. He emphasized it was important to understand that some people are depraved beyond comprehension, devoid of remorse, pity or empathy. He referred to them as "amoebas", creatures who responded only to external stimuli; they move away from the uncomfortable and towards personal gratification with no moral compass.

The 37th had marched south into Czechoslovakia when the war ended on May 6, 1945. The 37th participated in the task of disarming the Wehrmacht and set up shop in Bavaria as part of the occupation forces on May 27, 1945.

As the war wound to a close, Giuseppe and Paul were in charge of a group of German POW's. The first thing Giuseppe did in his official capacity of warden was find some useful activity for the prisoners in his charge. He appropriated brooms, shovels, and wheelbarrows and one block at a time his prison crew cleared debris from the streets. When it came their turn to leave, one the German officers approached Giuseppe. He said, "Here is a souvenir for you." He reached in his boot and pulled out a Browning automatic pistol and handed it to him for a keepsake.

Car modified to burn wood instead of petrol

The war was over.

For the first time in six years, Giuseppe was free to go wherever he wanted. It was time for Giuseppe to go home. But sometimes "home" isn't as clear-cut as you would think.

In the early spring of 1946, Giuseppe used his last army pass to visit his family. At the end of the war, practically nothing worked in Europe. Railroad tracks and bridges were destroyed. There were no trains. Giuseppe hired a local driver to make the journey. There was no petrol. The car had been modified to burn wood instead.

They had to depart from the army base at 4 o'clock in the morning, since it would take over 10 hours to cover the 600 kilometers from Bavaria to Cittadella considering the conditions of the roads, the limited speed of the car and frequent stops to reload wood. About 10 kilometers from his destination, as they were making their last refueling stop, Giuseppe's nephew Gian Paulo chanced to ride past on his bicycle. After recognizing each other and an excited greeting, Gian Paulo said that he was going ahead to tell everyone that he was only minutes away. Giuseppe protested that he would ruin the surprise. Gian Paulo said, "No it won't. No one will believe me." Gian Paulo leapt onto the bicycle, peddling furiously towards the ancient walled city. He easily outpaced the asthmatic motor car, racing towards the south gate of the fortress, the bicycle shuddering wildly over the cobble stones, ringing the bicycle bell furiously and shouting, "Nona! Nono!

Come quickly! It's Zio Beppe! It's Zio Beppe!" People spilled from the houses out into the street. His grandparents ran from the door of their house. "Are you alright Gian Paulo? What's wrong?"

Minutes later the asthmatic truck wheezed to a stop in front of Giuseppe's house. Seventy years later Gian Paulo still remembers the excitement of Giuseppe's arrival. He remembers his crisp American military uniform, replete with medals. It was as joyous a reunion as the one that awaits us in heaven. Mother, father, and sisters' cheeks wet with tears like meadows after a spring shower. Family and friends crowded into the tiny house; people brought food, beer, wine, grappa. People talking, shouting, singing.

After several days visiting with his family, he made the return trip to his base. He paid the driver with cartons of American cigarettes; the de facto currency of the time. He left several more cartons in the bedroom in his parents' house. They would purchase several months worth of food and other necessities.

He spent his free time over the next several days alone hiking though the Bavarian forest. For the last half dozen years, some government official decided every detail of his life from what he had for breakfast to where he went to sleep. Now he had unlimited freedom. He could be transported to any place on earth. He thought about the brief, awkward meeting at the Gloucester Detention Center and the letter with the memorized address that initiated a chain of correspondence that floated back and forth for years like the shuttlecock in a languorous game of badminton. A correspondence tethered at one end in Philadelphia, the opposite node following Giuseppe from

Gloucester to Ellis Island, Belgium and Germany. Letters filled with affection and hope.

Of all the forces that make for a better world, none is as powerful as hope. With hope, one can think, one can work, one can dream. A letter from a friend or lover turns a cold, wet day into a joyous one. If you have hope, you have everything. Nothing brings more hope to a prisoner or soldier than a letter. Every day in prison or the army begins with the anticipation of mail call. Of all the hand crafted gifts that one can bestow, none is so cherished as a letter.

Charlotte and Giuseppe were very private about this aspect of their lives. Of all of those letters, only one small scrap remains. Charlotte's sister Jackie was in her early teens at the time. Sixty years later she recalls the stack of letters bound with a white satin ribbon in her sister's room. She confessed to tip-toeing into Charlotte's room to peek at them. They were "hot," definitely not appropriate reading for a teenager, which only enhanced their allure. Each began with "My Dearest Lotus Flower…"

When the officer in charge asked Giuseppe where he wanted to be mustered out, he replied "How close can you get me to Philadelphia?" The officer scribbled some information on the form, pounded it firmly with a red rubber stamp, and handed him the papers.

***

July 28, 1946 was a mild cloudless afternoon in Philadelphia. At the house on 15th Street, a light breeze gently billowed the lace curtains at the open windows. The shades were pulled down half way to block the brilliant afternoon sun.

"Violet, did you borrow my green pillbox hat?"

"No. Ask mom if she's seen it."

"Charlotte, for heaven's sake, it's in the dresser drawer next to your gloves. Is Lillian going with you?"

"Yes. Lillian will be here any minute."

"When is this man's train due in?"

"Just after three o'clock. When are Conrad and Daddy coming home?"

"They're leaving work early. Don't fret; dinner will be ready when you get back."

"What are you making?"

"If this man's from Veneto he'll like lamb with polenta. Lillian's boyfriend, Clem, is coming and Conrad will be here with Lea."

"Hurry, Lillian's at the door now."

"Great. How's my lipstick?"

"It's perfect, perfect. Now go, you don't want to be late."

"How's my hair?"

It's perfect, already. Now go!"

Charlotte flew out the door and down the steps like a whirlwind, the screen door slamming shut behind her, Lillian in her wake. They turned up the sidewalk towards the Broad Street Subway Station.

DioMira watched until she disappeared around the corner at the end of the block. She said to her other daughter, "Violet, if that young man doesn't have his sorry ass on that train I don't know what I'll do with that girl."

Charlotte and Lillian descended the concrete steps to the subway station, the day's heat melting into cool dampness in the concrete tunnel descending to the train platform. Charlotte asked, "What do you think, Lil? How do I look?"

"Relax, you're perfect. You look more beautiful than ever." And she was. Even in the dim sepia colored light on the subway platform, she was radiant. She was wearing a black calf length circle skirt, a close fitting white jacket, and a short pearl necklace, topped with a pillbox hat with netting that just covered her blue eyes.

The subway squealed to a stop next to the platform and the doors slid open with a subdued hiss of compressed air. The girls boarded the closest car and the train rumbled away into the dark tunnel, red and green signal lights tearing by just outside the window. On the subway ride Lillian chided, "Now don't be making a spectacle of yourself in the station when you see this guy. I remember the last time you two were together."

"Now Lillian, that was years ago."

In just under a half hour the subway arrived at 30th Street Station. The girls climbed the concrete steps, emerging from the dark tunnel into the bright August sunlight that just broke through the clouds.

"Charlotte, have you considered the possibility that this guy might not even show up today?"

"No. He wrote and said he's going to be here. I know it."

"After so many years, do you even remember what he looks like?"

The cavernous station was nearly deserted in mid-afternoon. The café was empty except for an elderly couple sipping tea. The Negro Red Caps stood leaning against their empty luggage carts. Sunlight poured in through the station windows as Charlotte and Lillian watched the message board announce the coming and going of trains from different parts of the country. A pair of wrens darted back and forth among the chandeliers. The hands on the giant clock over the message board slowly inched forward.

They heard the train approaching, huffing like a marathon runner, whistle screaming. A minute later Charlotte felt the floor tremble as the locomotive rumbled alongside the platform below the waiting room, the engine exhaling white smoke that curled up from the stairwell like incense from the censer in church.

After what seemed like an eternity, people began to emerge from the stairwell, just one or two at first, then gradually swelling to a tide of bodies. Charlotte scanned each face looking for a hint of recognition. Then a man in uniform appeared; before she could even register the face she recognized the confident authority in the way he walked, she took a few tentative steps towards him and he saw her and he dropped his duffle bag and ran towards her and she quickened her pace. Wordlessly, they threw their arms around each other and kissed each other shamelessly as the station receded in the distance and the passengers and the Red Caps and the ticket clerks all disappeared, the hands on the big clock froze in place and there wasn't anything in the universe but each other and the only other thing was Charlotte's hair brushing their cheeks and the scent of her perfume. Each knew, in that moment, they would love each other always.

11

COURTSHIP

The wheel of life goes full circle. After the war, the Allies repatriated the Conte Biancamano to Italy. She was refurbished and returned to passenger service in the North Atlantic. Giuseppe's brother-in-law Ettorre emerged from his hermitage at Bella Vista. A modern day Rip Van Winkle, it  was as if he had simply drifted off to sleep one night and woke up a decade later. He returned to his former post at his desk in the Purser's office.

But Giuseppe knew things had changed. In the new egalitarian post-war society, the ostentatious display of wealth that was the raison d'être for the grand liners was now considered unseemly. Working class men who had fought in the war and women who had manned the production lines at home had a new sense of their own worth. If first class was beyond their means, they weren't about to tolerate being assigned to second or third class anything. The stately liners were in their twilight.

Giuseppe had no desire to resume life at sea. He was content in his adopted city of Philadelphia. He rented a room from Charlotte's Zia Rica, who had recently joined the family migration from Sheppton. She lived one block south of the house on 15th street. In classic Tyrolean tradition, John Tamea made a few discrete enquiries at work and in a few days Giuseppe had a job at the railcar factory working alongside John and Frank.

Charlotte and Giuseppe were inseparable. Giuseppe dined with Charlotte's family almost every night. On weekends they went to movies or a nightclub. They visited the museums. On winter evenings they braved swirling snow flurries to go to the Opera at the Academy of music, sitting in the cheap seats in the top level. Sometimes they would just spend an afternoon walking in Fairmount Park.

Then a letter from Ettorre arrived. The Conte Biancamano was scheduled to dock in New York in a few months. Joe replied and arranged to meet his brother-in-law in New York. He invited his girlfriend and her family to join him. Charlotte unhesitatingly said

John Tamea, Giuseppe and Ettorre in Central Park

"Yes!"

Charlotte's father and her younger sister Jackie accepted the invitation to join the adventure and act as chaperones. Thus it was a party of four that boarded the morning train at 30th Street Station bound for a three day hiatus in New York City.

The days were warm and sultry but Charlotte and Jackie looked as cool and bright as iced cupcakes in their white summer dresses. They rode the ferry across the Hudson River to the Statute of Liberty which provided a refreshing breeze and a respite from the heat of the city.

At Liberty Island, Jackie flirted with a group of Eagle scouts who were touring New York. John was basking in the simple pleasure of being off work for a few days. Charlotte and Joe walked around the Statue of Liberty holding hands. Ellis Island sat silent in the background, pigeons fluttered through the broken windows.

The next day they met Ettorre at the dock. He gave his visitors a cook's tour of the ship, the elaborate dining rooms and lounges, the ballroom, the beauty salon and barber shop, the jewelry stores and the movie theater.

They had dinner at a small restaurant in Little Italy that Giuseppe remembered from years prior when he lived nearby on LeRoy Street. Weeks before he had written to the couple that owned the restaurant to reserve a table.

They dined in a open air garden enclosed by a brick wall with a fountain in the wall at the far end of the garden. The fading sunlight cast a pink glow on the white linen tablecloths. Each table was set with a bouquet of summer flowers whose scent fused with the smell of rosemary emanating from the kitchen. Giuseppe and Charlotte held hands across the table, sometimes talking, sometimes laughing, and sometimes whispering to each other, Charlotte blushing at regular intervals. As shadows from the adjacent buildings quietly swept away the broken fragments of sunlight, waiters lit candles on each table. The candle light gave a warm buttery glow to Charlotte's white summer dress, and her deep blue eyes shone as bright as her amethyst earrings. Giuseppe and Charlotte tried exotic appetizers, took turns feeding each other morsels of food, and locked eyes with each other. Fireflies floated among the diners, searching for their lovers with their lamps.

A few days later Ettorre wrote to Joe's family that they would soon have a beautiful loving daughter-in-law.

A few years later in another story of improbable love, Jackie married a farmer from Winchester, Virginia, where she moved with her new husband. Now this former city girl wakes each morning to the crowing of her rooster. Every spring a blizzard of apple blossom petals from the surrounding orchards blankets her yard to mark the passing of another winter. But sixty years later she still vividly recalls her trip to New York, and her sister's divine happiness on a July evening. Her recollection of that summer evening provided this part of our story.

Giuseppe and Charlotte spent a blissful year dating, discovering Philadelphia, New York, and each other. This was followed by a year-long engagement in which they made a graceful transition from friendship to a deep and profound love that endured for decades.

They were married on a brisk Saturday in November 1947 in Charlotte's North Philadelphia parish church.

12

EPILOGUE

And They Lived Happily Ever After.

When Giuseppe returned from the war he wasn't a hyphenated anything. He was American. He introduced himself as Joe. He spoke English, albeit with a pronounced accent that persisted for the rest of his life. He wore American suits (with Italian shoes).

He worked for a Pump Company as a machinist. Yet, Joseph aspired to more than factory work. Mass production may have ended the craft tradition, but the experience in his father's shop imbued him with an innate desire to make things that were both beautiful and functional. Cashing in on the G.I. Bill, he enrolled at the Philadelphia College of Art, attending school during the day and working full-time on the night shift. He graduated in 1954 with a degree in Industrial Design.

Joseph and Charlotte bought a row home in Philadelphia. The city had everything they needed: opera house, museums and public transit. Despite having driven a tank across Europe, Joseph shunned the motor car as a mode of personal transportation, preferring the trolley car and subway.

During the post-war decade their contemporaries worked furiously so they could move to Levittown and buy a new Chevrolet station wagon and a color TV. Joseph and Charlotte never aspired to any such thing. They cherished their Bohemian urban life together. In their frame of reference, filling their home with original paintings and sculpture was more important than a television.

In July of 1951, Joseph and Charlotte were blessed with a son, David, followed seven years later by a daughter, Eve.

Weekdays in the Gardellin household were patterened on life on the Comte Biancamano and the army. By first-grade David's weekdays began with Inspection at 7:00 AM: Hair combed, teeth brushed, shoes shined, pants creased, white shirt pressed and starched and tie fastened properly. By 8:15 he was at his desk at St Athanasius School.

Every weekday at precisely 5:20 PM the green and white P.T.C. bus stopped at the corner of Rodney and Mayland Streets. The mechanical doors swung open and Joseph stepped off. David stopped playing and ran to the bus stop and threw his arms around his father and they walked home hand-in-hand. Mother had dinner on the table. After dinner, Joseph supervised homework; children recited times-tables and the Baltimore Catechism. After homework, Joseph read to his children.

On Fridays evenings, mother hung up the apron and the family went for dinner at a small storefront Italian restaurant. Water spouted form a fountain in the front of the restaurant and there were pictures of Venice on the walls and Joe would tell us about Venice and he chatted with the waiters in Italian.

Weekend visitors originated from everywhere in the world: Italy, Germany, India, Ukraine, Japan, Argentina and Columbia. For the better part of my high school years almost every weekend the house was filled with our Indian friends.

Joseph and Charlotte saw their children happily married. They saw their granddaughter Diomira blossom into a beautiful young woman.

For decades after the war, Joseph periodically received letters from friends from his days at Bella Vista, invariably addressed to "My Dear Mister Bull of the Chicken".

I have no reliable proof that God permits us to choose our parents. But I know that, given the choice, I would unhesitatingly have chosen Giuseppe Gardellin and Charlotte Tamea for my father and mother.

Acknowledgements

Special thanks to my wife Grace for her unflagging support and enthusiasm for this project.

Special thanks also to my sister Eve for her support and for help keeping various relatives in their correct position in the family tree and for filling in large portions of the story that that were missing from my recollection.

The bulk of this story relies on oral family tradition, but there are sections of story that merit specific mention:

Details of the history of Fort Missoula and Nick Collaer and pictures of the Fort Missoula internment camp are from the book "An Alien Place", and were made available through the generous permission of the author, Carol Bulger Van

Valkenburg and her publisher Pictorial Histories Publishing Co in Missoula MT.

The photographs depicting the 37th Battalion during WWII were discovered in my father's papers when he passed away. It's possible they were taken by my father who acquired a camera during the war. However, the high technical quality of the photographs suggests to me that they were most likely taken by a professional photojournalist in the company of the Battalion.

I frequently would overhear my father and Paul recounting their exploits during the war, but I verified dates and locations for the 37th battalion using Wikipedia:

http://en.wikipedia.org/wiki/37th_Armor_Regiment_(United_States)

I verified dates of my father's capture, internment, and enlistment in the army by a Freedom of Information request to the CIA who provided me with a copy of his OSS file. This file also included the letters shown in the text and the letters written by Father Menager in his campaign to secure my father's release when he was incarcerated at the Gloucester INS detention center.

Made in the
USA
Middletown, DE